how2become

KS3 ENGLISH IS EASY

(READING — SHAKESPEARE)

THE
REVISION
SERIES

www.How2Become.com

As part of this product you have also received FREE access to online tests that will help you to pass Key Stage 3 ENGLISH
(Reading – Shakespeare).

To gain access, simply go to:

www.PsychometricTestsOnline.co.uk

Get more products
for passing any test at:

www.How2Become.com

Orders: Please contact How2Become Ltd, Suite 14, 50 Churchill Square Business Centre, Kings Hill, Kent ME19 4YU.

You can order through Amazon.co.uk under ISBN 9781911259008, via the website www.How2Become.com or through Gardners.com.

ISBN: 9781911259008

First published in 2016 by How2Become Ltd.

Copyright © 2016 How2Become.

Typeset for How2Become Ltd by Anton Pshinka.

Disclaimer

CONTENTS

THE
REVISION
SERIES

UNDERSTANDING THE CURRICULUM

THE NATIONAL CURRICULUM

State-funded schools are governed by a set curriculum of 'core' subjects which must form part of children's timetables. These core subjects are essential for providing key knowledge and skills; which in turn will help us to produce well-rounded and educated citizens.

In Key Stage 3 (ages 11-14), the core subjects that must be taught in schools include the following:

- **English**
- **Maths**
- **Science**
- **Art and Design**
- **Citizenship**
- **Computing**
- **Design and Technology**
- **Languages**
- **Geography**
- **History**
- **Music**
- **Physical Education**

All schools, Key Stage 1 to Key Stage 4, must also teach Religious Studies to their students; and from the age of 11, children will also be taught Sex Education. However, parents are given the option of pulling their children out from Religious Studies and Sex Education.

THE IMPORTANCE OF ENGLISH

Students are taught the importance of English via spoken language, reading, writing and vocabulary. Not only is this a core subject which all students are required to undertake, but this subject is an integral part of other school subjects. Children will need to have a strong grasp of the English Language, and this will prove vital if they are to be successful across their school subjects.

The fundamental aims of the English subject include:

- Reading with fluency and ease;

- Demonstrating a good understanding of the English Language;

- Highlighting the importance of reading, and allowing students to read for both pleasure and academia;

- Appreciating the English Language and its heritage;

- Acquiring a strong English vocabulary to improve students' knowledge in regards to reading, writing and listening;

- Writing strong literature; and adapting their writing and language in order to demonstrate its purpose, context and audience;

- Improving children's confidence in their English abilities, allowing them to become competent in the English Language via verbal and written communication.

In Key Stage 3, the English subject focuses on four main 'disciplines':

- **Reading;**
- **Writing;**
- **Grammar and Vocabulary;**
- **Spoken English.**

The aforementioned disciplines are all used to teach students vital skills for both academia and the outside world.

READING AND WRITING

Reading and writing skills form the very basic skills that every person should obtain from an early age.

Reading is great for students since it allows them to read for pleasure as well as for information. The ability to read is also necessary across other school subjects and therefore it is important that students are able to read fluently and effectively.

Writing is a great skill which can be altered to reflect different contexts, purposes and audiences. In Key Stage 3, students are required to write different literary texts, for different purposes. Thus, this requires a strong level of knowledge regarding vocabulary and grammar.

GRAMMAR AND VOCABULARY

Students in Key Stage 3 will need to extend knowledge which was obtained in Key Stage 2.

Teachers will need to enhance students' knowledge by teaching them the importance of grammar, punctuation and spelling. These key areas allow students to not only analyse literary texts, but also improve their own writing style.

Linguistically, students will need to develop a strong understanding of English terminology, and learn how this can be applied to literary texts. This includes learning the ability to use appropriate vocabulary, understanding the meaning of words and phrases, and learning how to analyse, practice and apply literary techniques to their own work.

SPOKEN ENGLISH

Not only is written communication an important aspect of the English Language, but the ability to speak fluent English is just as vital.

Spoken English is used every day, in a range of different contexts. Developing a person's speaking skills will allow for well-rounded citizens who have the ability to communicate effectively.

Speaking skills allow students to become more confident at speaking out loud, and to engage with the English Language competently.

Having a strong understanding of the English Language will allow students to become fluent in written and spoken English. This will allow them to communicate effectively with the world around them, thus allowing children to become engaged in cultural, social and economic issues, and intellectual debates.

ENGLISH SUBJECT CONTENT

Below we have broken down the aims and objectives of each 'discipline' for the subject. This will hopefully give you some idea of what will be assessed, and how you can improve different areas in your reading, writing and speaking abilities.

READING

Pupils will be taught how to:

❑ Develop an appreciation of the English language.
❑ Engage with a variety of literary texts including:
  - *Non-fiction, fiction, plays and poetry. Texts that cover a wide range of genres, eras, authors, styles and narratives.*
  - *Reading books for pleasure and academia.*
  - *Understanding the importance of Shakespeare's works.*
❑ Engage with challenging texts by:
  - *Learning new vocabulary, grammar and literary techniques.*
  - *Analysing key words and phrases.*
  - *Making inferences and assumptions based on the information provided.*
  - *Knowing the meaning behind the text, including the purpose, audience and context.*
❑ Read critically:
  - *Recognising different literary techniques.*
  - *Analysing narration, characterisation, style, themes and genre.*
  - *Comparing two or more texts (cross-examination).*
  - *Understanding meaning through figurative language, word choices, structure and conventions.*

WRITING

<u>Pupils will be taught how to:</u>

❑ Write with fluency, ease and control.
❑ Write a range of different literary texts including:
  ▪ *Strong, persuasive, narrative essays.*
  ▪ *Short stories, plays, poetry.*
  ▪ *Imaginative writing.*
  ▪ *Formal letters.*
  ▪ *Scripts and presentations.*
❑ Plan, draft and proofread writing:
  ▪ *Plan and draft your ideas. Think about:*
    ○ *Characters, narrative, themes, motives, style, context, audience, purpose.*
  ▪ *Carefully choosing grammar and understanding the importance of vocabulary.*
  ▪ *Structuring your writing format in a clear and concise manner.*
  ▪ *Understanding the importance of audience, and how your writing can be influential.*
❑ Be original and creative.
❑ Use the English language in a way that is expressive, creative, informative, imaginative or personal.

SPOKEN ENGLISH

<u>Pupils will be taught how to:</u>

❑ Verbally communicate to a high standard by:
  ▪ *Speaking confidently, persuasively and effectively.*
❑ Improve their speaking skills by engaging with particular grammar and vocabulary:
  ▪ *Understanding what type of spoken English they should use and in what context.*
  ▪ *Understanding how to get their point across in the best possible way.*
❑ Participate in verbal debates, discussions and presentations.
❑ Improve on speaking skills such as volume, tone, enthusiasm and interaction.

GRAMMAR AND VOCABULARY

Pupils will be taught how to:

☐ Improve on pre-existing grammar and vocabulary skills taught in Key Stage 2.
☐ Understand the importance of grammar:
  - *How this creates meaning.*
  - *The impact this has on the audience.*
☐ Analyse key words and phrases:
  - *Why they are used.*
  - *The meaning behind them.*
  - *What is the author implying/inferring?*
☐ Understand what grammar and vocabulary to use. Think about:
  - *What kind of literary text they are writing/reading.*
  - *What do words mean and how can they be interpreted?*
  - *Is it a formal or informal piece of literary text?*

English is not only a core subject, but a topic that impacts upon every aspect of our daily lives. As you can see, it is imperative that students are able to engage with the English Language, in order to improve on vital skills and knowledge.

USING THIS GUIDE

This guide focuses specifically on Key Stage 3 English Reading (Shakespeare). This book will focus on the basics that every child will need to know, to ensure top marks across the English subject.

REMEMBER – It's really important that you have a good reading ability, as this will help across all school subjects.

HOW WILL I BE ASSESSED?

In Years 7, 8 and 9, children will be assessed based on Levels. These 3 years do not count towards anything, and are simply a reflection of progression and development. Key Stage 3 (Years 7, 8 and 9) are schooling years which determine whether or not pupils are meeting the minimum requirements. These 3 years are integral for preparing pupils for their GCSEs (which will begin in Year 10).

Although these years do not count towards any final results, they do go a long way to deciphering which GCSEs you will pick up in Year 10. For example, if you were excelling in Art and Design in KS3, you could consider taking this subject at GCSE. The subjects that you choose at GCSE will impact upon your future aspirations, including further education and career opportunities.

You will be monitored and assessed throughout these schooling years, via the following:

- Ongoing teacher assessments;
- Term progress reports;
- Summative assessments at the end of each academic year.

By the end of Key Stage 3, pupils are expected to achieve Levels 5 or 6.

THE
REVISION
SERIES

INCREASE YOUR CHANCES

Below is a list of GOLDEN NUGGETS that will help YOU and your CHILD to prepare for Key Stage 3 English.

Golden Nugget 1 – Revision timetables

When it comes to revising, preparation is key. That is why you need to sit down with your child and come up with an efficient and well-structured revision timetable.

It is important that you work with your child to assess their academic strengths and weaknesses, in order to carry out these revision sessions successfully.

TIP – Focus on their weaker areas first!

TIP – Create a weekly revision timetable to work through different subject areas.

TIP – Spend time revising with your child. Your child will benefit from your help and this is a great way for you to monitor their progress.

Golden Nugget 2 – Understanding the best way your child learns

There are many different ways to revise when it comes to exams, and it all comes down to picking a way that your child will find most useful.

Below is a list of the common learning styles that you may want to try with your child:

- **Visual** – the use of pictures and images to remember information.

- **Aural** – the use of sound and music to remember information.

- **Verbal** – the use of words, in both speech and writing, to understand information.

- **Social** – working together in groups.

- **Solitary** – working and studying alone.

Popular revision techniques include: *mind mapping, flash cards, making notes, drawing flow charts,* and *diagrams*. You could instruct your child on how to turn diagrams and pictures into words, and words into diagrams. Try as many different methods as possible, to see which style your child learns from the most.

> ***TIP*** *– Work out what kind of learner your child is. What method will they benefit from the most?*
>
> ***TIP*** *– Try a couple of different learning aids and see if you notice a change in your child's ability to understand what is being taught.*

Golden Nugget 3 – Break times

Allow your child plenty of breaks when revising.

It's really important not to overwork your child.

> ***TIP*** *– Practising for 10 to 15 minutes per day will improve your child's reading ability.*
>
> ***TIP*** *– Keep in mind that a child's retention rate is usually between 30 to 50 minutes. Any longer than this, and your child will start to lose interest.*

Golden Nugget 4 – Practice, practice and more practice!

Purchase past practice papers. Although the curriculum will have changed for 2016, practice papers are still a fantastic way for you to gain an idea of how your child is likely to be tested.

Golden Nugget 5 – Variety is key!

Make sure that your child reads a VARIETY of different literary texts. Broadening their understanding of different genres, styles and formats will help them prepare effectively for reading comprehension.

> *TIP – Take your child to a library and let them discover different types of books. This will greatly increase their understanding of different literary styles.*

Golden Nugget 6 – Improve their confidence

Encourage your child to communicate verbally, as well as in writing. This will allow them to improve their confidence and improve their spoken English.

> *TIP – Have discussions and debates in order to encourage your child to open up and discuss their views.*
>
> *TIP – Try and get your child to deliver presentations to family members and friends. This will really help to improve their confidence.*

Golden Nugget 7 – Stay positive!

The most important piece of preparation advice we can give you, is to make sure that your child is positive and relaxed about these tests.

Don't let assessments worry you, and certainly don't let them worry your child.

> *TIP – Make sure the home environment is as comfortable and relaxed as possible for your child.*

Golden Nugget 8 – Answer the easier questions first

A good tip to teach your child is to answer all the questions they find easiest first. That way, they can swiftly work through the paper, before attempting the questions they struggle with.

TIP – Get your child to undergo a practice paper. Tell them to fill in the answers that they find the easiest first. That way, you can spend time helping your child with the questions they find more difficult.

Spend some time working through the questions they find difficult and make sure that they know how to work out the answer.

Golden Nugget 9 – Make sure they refer back to the text

One of the biggest mistakes a child can make in their English exams, is that they don't refer back to the text. All of the answers can be found in the text, therefore they should support their answers with information taken from the passage, as opposed to relying on their memory.

Golden Nugget 10 – Understanding translations

The next section is a list of translations to help you understand some of the words Shakespeare used in his literary works.

Sit down with your child and learn as many of these words as you can.

TIP – Why not make your child's learning fun? Write down all of the Elizabethan terms and cut them out individually. Do the same for the modern-day translation.

Get your child to try and match the Elizabethan term with the modern-day term. Keep playing this game until they get them all right!

Golden Nugget 11 – Check out our other revision resources

We have a range of other English resources to help you prepare for EVERY element of KS3 English.

Of course, we cannot provide you with all of Shakespeare's unusual Elizabethan words. However, we thought we would provide you with some of the most popular words and translations, in order to become familiar with the kind of language Shakespeare used.

We have also provided space for you to fill in words yourself to see whether or not you are able to translate old-fashioned English into modern-day English. As you read through works of Shakespeare, if there are any words you are unsure of, write them down and get a friend, parent or teacher to help you translate it.

Remember to use this glossary when revising to ensure you know what Shakespeare is talking about.

MODERN DAY	ELIZABETHAN
Afraid	Afeard
Aware	Acknown
Away	Hence
Banished	Banish'd
Before	Ere
Beg	Pray
Chase (romantically)	Woo
Come here	Come hither
Curse	Plague
Days	-morrow
Desire	Will
Does	Doth
Enemy	Foe
Escaped	'scap'd
Farewell	Adieu
Go	Hie
Go away	Avaunt
Has	Hath
Have	Hast

Here	Hither
Indeed	Marry
Inferiors	Sirrah
I think	Methinks
It is	'tis
Ignore	Shun
Kill	Dispatch
Listen	Hark
Misery	Woe
Never	Ne'r
No	Nay
Nothing	Nought
Often	Oft
Order	Charge
Pay attention	Mark
Quickly	Apace
Remember	Bethink
Sad	Heavy
Soon	Anon
There	Thither
To which	Whereto
Were	Wast
Why	Wherefore
Wished	Wish'd
Yes	Aye
You	Thou; thee
You are	Thou art
You should	Thou should'st
Your	Thy

MODERN DAY	ELIZABETHAN

THE
REVISION
SERIES

EXPLORING WILLIAM SHAKESPEARE

WILLIAM SHAKESPEARE

LIVING IN SHAKESPEAREAN TIMES

Obviously, there are many differences between the era in which Shakespeare was writing, and now.

Shakespeare's writing was heavily influenced by what life was like. This enabled him to appeal to his audiences, by conveying similar imagery and values which were recognisable.

The key areas that Shakespeare paid particular attention to when writing are listed below.

GOVERNMENT

- For the majority of his life, Shakespeare grew up writing under the reigning monarch of Queen Elizabeth I.
- King James I ruled after her.

RELIGION

- England was a Christian country.
- Almost everyone believed in God and went to church.
- Many people believed in witchcraft, magic and ghosts.
- No-one divorced in this era.

WOMEN

- Women had no rights.
- They had to obey what their father (and/or husband) told them.
- Women had no career opportunities.
- They were often forced into arranged marriages.
- Even if the woman was the eldest, the first eldest brother would inherit everything.

WILLIAM SHAKESPEARE

EDUCATION

- Boys (from the age of 4) would go to school to learn to read and write.
- They would also learn prayers, teachings of the Church, and working with numbers.
- Grammar schools would focus on Latin, translations and writing.
- Girls would stay at home and learn to be domesticated (cook, sew, music). Only a few girls would learn to read and write.

HEALTH

- Diseases were prominent around the city of London.
- The Black Death (also known as the Plague) wiped out thousands of civilians.
- Many children died from the disease, including Shakespeare's son, Hamnet.

CLASS

- At the time of writing, society was divided into different **classes**.
- These classes defined people's wealth and status, which ultimately formed a hierarchy which people would follow.
- The nobles (considered the very richest of people) were called 'lords' and 'ladies'. They were the ruling class, which had influence over what the monarchy did.
- Just beneath the nobles, were the gentry. These people were rich enough to survive off their own wealth, but did not have titles within society.
- Shakespeare himself was raised as a middle class citizen. The middle class consisted of yeomen, merchants and craftsmen. Whilst they were not wealthy, they lived comfortably, and their children would have gone to school.
- The lower class worked for the superiors in society. The lower class had little money, but were still able to attend the theatre.

WILLIAM SHAKESPEARE

FEATURES OF SHAKESPEARE'S WORK

Shakespeare used a range of literary techniques in order to appeal to his readers / audiences.

There are three main areas that you should focus on when reading Shakespeare:

- Language
- Characters
- Themes

LANGUAGE

Many people struggle to understand the works of Shakespeare, because his writing style and language is extremely different to ours.

The use of old-fashioned language made it difficult for readers to interpret, but these words and phrases were often worked out by understanding the rest of the script.

For example:

The below extract is the opening from Othello.

> **RODERIGO**
> Tush, <u>never tell me</u>! I take it much unkindly
> That though, Iago, who <u>hast</u> had my purse
> As if the strings were thine shouldst know of <u>this</u>.
>
> *Don't try and make me believe that*
>
> *Have*
>
> *Talking about the elopement of Othello and Desdemona*

Getting used to the language is difficult, but with more practice, this will become easier.

Remember, you don't have to understand every word in order to understand what is being said. Some of the words are simply missing letters, whilst others are words that you might not have heard of!

WILLIAM SHAKESPEARE

You will need to be able to translate what is being said, in order to analyse what is being said.

Some things to look out for:

Words that you may not recognise or used in a different context to how it would be used today.

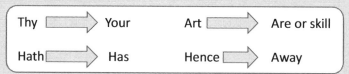

Thy ⇒ Your   Art ⇒ Are or skill

Hath ⇒ Has   Hence ⇒ Away

The language used was often quite 'wordy'. Words and phrases were often swapped around which makes it tricky to work out what is actually being said.

When you read Shakespeare's plays, it is important to read straight into the next line (unless there is a full stop or other punctuation mark).

In a lot of Shakespeare's works, he used poetic devices in his dialogue. Poetry was often spoken by the characters who were wealthy; whereas slang and normal language were spoken by the commoners.

> Full fathom five thy father lies;
> Of is bones are coral made;
> Those are pearls that were his eyes:
> Nothing of him that doth fade.
>
> *The Tempest*

Shakespeare used language to emphasise religious, biblical, medical, legal and sexual references.

WILLIAM SHAKESPEARE

CHARACTERS

Characters play a crucial role in the works of Shakespeare. They are often conveyed to the audience in a particular way, in order to create different emotions and ideas about each character.

<u>When you read about characters, you need to consider the following:</u>

- *How do they act?*
- *What is their role in the narrative?*
- *What do they get up to?*
- *How do they speak?*
- *What is their relationships like with other characters?*
- *How does Shakespeare want you to feel about that character?*

<u>Take a look at the representation of a few characters from Romeo and Juliet:</u>

CHARACTER	REPRESENTATION
Romeo	• Impulsive, immature, devoted, passionate • His dialogue towards Juliet is very poetic, deep and meaningful
Juliet	• Naïve, innocent, devoted • Lack of freedom (compared to Romeo) • Shows courage and independence
Friar Lawrence	• Friend to both Romeo and Juliet • Civic-minded • Tries to create union between both families by marrying the lovers
The Nurse	• Sentimental character • Confidant to Juliet • A comical character

WILLIAM SHAKESPEARE

THEMES

What is the play about? What is the overall theme of the play?

Shakespeare wrote loads of plays, each of which focussed on different key themes. These themes were all considered relevant to the time in which Shakespeare was writing.

There are three types of Shakespearean plays:

1. Comedies
2. Tragedies
3. Histories

Comedies

- This is a different type of humour than what we find funny in today's world.
- Most Shakespearean comedies offer dramatic storylines, alongside their underlying humour.
- Most comedies offer a happy ending.

Characteristics = struggle of young love, element of separation, mistaken identities, interwoven plotlines, use of puns and irony, and family conflict.

Tragedies

- Tend to be more serious, dramatic and tense.
- Usually involve death of main character/s.

Characteristics = social breakdown, isolation of main characters, ends in death, noble characters who are brought down by their flaws, and no escape from the drama.

Histories

- Focus on English monarchs including King John, Richard II, Henry VIII and loads more.
- Dangers of civil war and conflict.
- Present a particular image of monarchs, although often considered as misrepresentations and inaccurate.

Characteristics = use of English monarchs to centre the storyline, glorify ancestors, depict monarchs in a particular way, and use conflict and tragedy to dramatise the narrative.

WILLIAM SHAKESPEARE

Below I have listed some common themes that appear across the works of Shakespeare.

Love	Forbidden love	Family	Friendship
Morals	Religion	Rivalry	Honour
Innocence	Revenge	Fate	Justice
Slavery	Magic	Betrayal	Forgiveness
Order	Retribution	Good vs. Evil	Deception

Can you think of what themes appear in what play?

Generally, plays will have more than one theme running through the narrative.

Some themes may be more obvious than others.

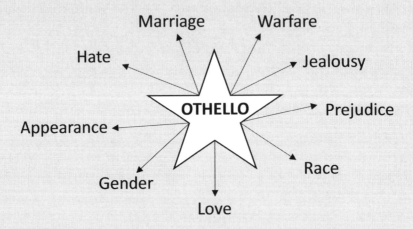

Marriage   Warfare

Hate   Jealousy

OTHELLO   Prejudice

Appearance

Gender   Race

Love

WILLIAM SHAKESPEARE

AUDIENCES

William Shakespeare's works appealed to the majority. Just like today, ticket prices were based on whereabouts you sat.

Shakespeare wanted to target a mass audience, from merchants and nobles, to poorer people.

When it comes to reading the works of Shakespeare, it is important that, as the reader, you are able to understand how Shakespeare appealed to his audience.

In his works, Shakespeare used language, imagery, themes, characters and narrative to appeal to his targeted audience. We will look at each of the aforementioned in more detail.

FUN FACTS!

- If the audience didn't like the play, they would throw apples at the actors.
- The only person who didn't go to the theatre was Queen Elizabeth I.
- People who stood to watch the play are called 'groundlings'. In the summer, they would be referred to as 'stinkards'.
- Merchants would buy tickets to sit in the boxes next to the stage.
- Nobles would buy seats on the stage because they could be seen by everyone.

THE
REVISION
SERIES

OTHELLO

(Analysing Plays)

OTHELLO

THE STORY OF OTHELLO

A story full of love, tragedy, suspicion and grief, *Othello* tells the story of a black man (Othello) who secretly marries a woman from one of the first noblest families (Desdemona).

As the play progresses, the audience visualise a change in Othello's personality. He is conveyed as being highly doubtful and suspicious as to whether his wife has been unfaithful to him. These suspicions are inculcated by the villain of the play, Iago.

CHARACTERS

Below I have outlined the main characters in the play, *Othello*.

When you read through the play, consider the following:

* *What is the purpose of each character?*
* *What role do they have in the play?*
* *How does Shakespeare want you to feel towards each character?*

OTHELLO	A Christian 'Moor'. The main protagonist who is the General of the armies in Venice. Living in a prejudiced society.
DESDEMONA	Othello's wife. Daughter of Venetian Senator, Brabantio. Married Othello in secret.
IAGO	Othello's ensign and villain of the play. His motifs throughout the play are questionable, and results in Othello doubting Desdemona's faithfulness.
EMILIA	Iago's wife. Desdemona's lady-in-waiting. Loyal to both. Her attitude towards men is different to that of Desdemona's.
BRABANTIO	Desdemona's father and Venetian Senator. He is less than impressed with her marriage to a black man.
CASSIO	Othello's lieutenant. Young, inexperienced soldier. Resented by Iago. Considered as having weaknesses for drink and women.
BIANCA	Cassio's mistress. A courtesan (prostitute) in Cyprus. Cassio plays with her emotions and promises to marry her.
RODERIGO	A jealous suitor of Desdemona. Constantly manipulated by Iago.

OTHELLO

THEMES

The main theme conveyed in the play *Othello* is jealousy. Shakespeare explores this theme via different characters.

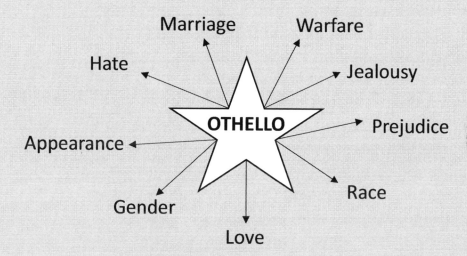

JEALOUSY = Iago makes Othello believe that his wife, Desdemona, has been unfaithful. Othello's jealousy continues to spiral out of control as the play comes to an end, resulting in the death of himself, his wife and others.

Jealousy is also portrayed in other characters. Iago is jealous of Cassio's position and authority in the military; Bianca is jealous about Cassio; and Iago shows jealousy towards Emilia.

RACE = the idea of a mixed race marriage would be frowned upon by the majority of people at the time this play was written. The racial language used to describe Othello would have been accepted by most, and considered the 'norm'. Whilst Shakespeare does draw upon racism, he attempts to challenge this by making Othello the hero and Iago the villain.

REALITY AND APPEARANCE = it is questionable as to what is real and what 'appears' to be real. Iago's attempt to convey truth and honesty is nothing more than a cover-up. The dramatic irony of Iago stating how men should be what they seem draws emphasis to this theme.

EXTRACTS

*This extract is taken from **Act I Scene I**. Iago is talking to Roderigo about Othello and Desdemona.*

IAGO

O sir, content you;
I follow him to serve my turn upon him:
We cannot all be masters, nor all masters
Cannot be truly follow'd. You shall mark
Many a duteous and knee-crooking knave,
That, doting on his own obsequious bondage,
Wears out his time much like his master's ass,
For nought but provender, and when he's old, cashier'd:
Whip me such honest knaves. Others there are
Who, trimm'd in forms and visages of duty,
Keep yet their hearts attending on themselves,
And, throwing but shows of service on their lords,
Do well thrive by them and when they have lined their coats,
Do themselves homage: these fellows have some soul,
And such a one do I profess myself. For, sir,
It is as sure as you are Roderigo,
Were I the Moor, I would not be Iago;
In following him, I follow but myself;
Heaven is my judge, not I for love and duty,
But seeming so, for my peculiar end:
For when my outward action doth demonstrate
The native act and figure of my heart
In compliment extern, 'tis not long after
But I will wear my heart upon my sleeve
For daws to peck at: I am not what I am.

*This extract is taken from **Act III Scene III**. Othello is showing his doubts towards Desdemona's faithfulness.*

OTHELLO
This fellow's of exceeding honesty
And knows all qualities, with a learned spirit,
Of human dealings. If I do prove her haggard,
Though that her jesses were my dear heart-strings,
I'd whistle her off and let her down the wind
To prey at fortune. Haply for I am black,
And have not those soft parts of conversation
That chamberers have, or for I am declined
Into the vale of years – yet that's not much –
She's gone, I am abused, and my relief
Must be to loathe her. O curse of marriage,
That we can call these delicate creatures ours
And not their appetites! I had rather be a toad
And live upon the vapour of a dungeon
Than keep a corner in the thing I love
For others' uses. Yet 'tis the plague of great ones,
Prerogativ'd are they less than the base;
'Tis destiny unshunnable, like death:
Even then this forked plague is fated to us
When we do quicken. Look where she comes.
    Enter Desdemona and Emilia
If she be false, O then heaven mocks itself!
I'll not believe't.

DESDEMONA
How now, my dear Othello?
Your dinner, and the generous islanders
By you invited, do attend your presence.

OTHELLO

I am to blame.

DESDEMONA

Why do you speak so faintly?

Are you not well?

OTHELLO

I have a pain upon my forehead here.

DESDEMONA

Faith, that's with watching; 'twill away again.

Let me but bind it hard, within this hour

It will be well.

OTHELLO

Your napkin is too little.

　　He puts the handkerchief from him, and drops it

Let it alone. Come, I'll go in with you.

DESDEMONA

I am very sorry that you are not well.

　　　　　　　　　　　　　　[Exeunt Othello and Desdemona]

*This extract is taken from **Act V Scene II**. Othello is psyching himself up to kill his wife, Desdemona.*

OTHELLO

It is the cause, it is the cause, my soul,
Let me not name it to you, you chaste stars!
It is the cause. Yet I'll not shed her blood;
Nor scar that whiter skin of hers than snow,
And smooth as monumental alabaster.
Yet she must die, else she'll betray more men.
Put out the light, and then put out the light:
If I quench thee, thou flaming minister,
I can again thy former light restore,
Should I repent me: but once put out thy light,
Thou cunning'st pattern of excelling nature,
I know not where is that Promethean heat
That can thy light relume. When I have pluck'd the rose
I cannot give it vital growth again.
It must needs wither: I'll smell it on the tree.
    He kisses her.
O balmy breath, that dost almost persuade
Justice to break her sword! One more, one more!
Be thus when thou art dead, and I will kill thee
And love thee after. One more, and this the last:
So sweet was ne'er so fatal. I must weep,
But they are cruel tears: this sorrow's heavenly –
It strikes where it doth love. She wakes.

DESDEMONA

Who's there? Othello?

PRACTICE QUESTIONS

*For questions 1-4, refer to **Act I Scene I.***

Question 1

How do the last two lines of Iago's dialogue reinforce his cunning and manipulative personality?

_____

_____

_____

_____

Question 2

What is Iago saying here? What theme is explored through the characterisation of Iago?

> "Were I the Moor, I would not be Iago; / In following him, I follow but myself; / Heaven is my judge, not I for love and duty, / But seeming so, for my peculiar end."

_____

_____

_____

Question 3

What does the following dialogue suggest about Iago's character?

> "I follow him to serve my turn upon him."

_____

_____

_____

Question 4

> *"In following him, I follow but myself;*
> *Heaven is my judge, not I for love and duty,*
> *But seeming so, for my peculiar end."*

Iago refers to heaven as being his judge for his manipulative behaviour. Why does Shakespeare do this?

_____

_____

_____

*For questions 5-8, refer to **Act III Scene III**.*

Question 5

What do you think Othello means by the handkerchief is "too little"? What does this suggest about their relationship?

_____

_____

_____

Question 6

Explain how Othello is blindsided by Iago's behaviour.

_____

_____

_____

_____

_____

_____

Question 7

What do you think the phrase "I'd whistle her off" means?

_____

_____

_____

Question 8

Using examples from the extract, explain how Iago's cunning plan of making Othello believe his wife has been unfaithful, is starting to work.

_____

_____

_____

_____

_____

_ _

*For questions 9-12, refer to **Act V Scene II**.*

_ _

Question 9

Shakespeare uses a metaphor to describe the appearance of Desdemona. Write the metaphor and explain how this conveys the idea of innocence and purity.

METAPHOR

_____

EXPLANATION

_____

_____

_____

Question 10

Give examples from Othello's dialogue which suggest his reservations about killing his wife.

_____

_____

_____

_____

_____

_____

Question 11

What is the main theme/s conveyed in Othello's dialogue? How does this relate to the overall narrative of *Othello*?

_____

_____

_____

_____

_____

_____

Question 12

Othello talks about a light. Describe what this light symbolises.

_____

_____

_____

_____

ESSAY QUESTIONS

1. One of the main themes Shakespeare highlights in *Othello* is the idea of doubt and betrayal. Using Othello's soliloquy from **Act III Scene III** and references from other Acts in the play, discuss the reasons why Othello suspects Desdemona of betrayal.

2. Explain and analyse the importance of the role of women in the play, *Othello*. What effect does this have on audiences in the Elizabethan era compared to modern day?

3. How is Iago represented throughout the play of *Othello*? Draw upon his relationship with other characters and how he is perceived by the audience.

THE
REVISION
SERIES

ROMEO
AND JULIET

(Analysing Plays)

ROMEO AND JULIET

THE STORY OF ROMEO AND JULIET

One of the most well-known plays about tragedy and love, *Romeo and Juliet* is a story based on a girl and boy (from two rival families) who fall in love. Despite their family feuds, they decide to marry in secret and run away together.

Juliet plans to fake her death, but with Romeo unaware of her plan, he kills himself next to her bedside. Juliet wakes up to find him dead, and decides to kill herself as well.

CHARACTERS

Below I have outlined the main characters in the play, *Romeo and Juliet*.

When you read through the play, consider the following:

- *What is the purpose of each character?*
- *What role do they have in the play?*
- *How does Shakespeare want you to feel towards each character?*

ROMEO	Son and heir of the Montague family – a family in a constant fight with the Capulet family. He goes all-out to demonstrate his love for Juliet.
JULIET	Daughter of Capulet and Lady Capulet, who begins knowing very little about love. Her love for Romeo continues to evolve. She entrusts Romeo and plans to run away and spend their lives together.
FRIAR LAWRENCE	Friend to Romeo and Juliet. Marries them in secret in hope to resolve the feud between their families.
MERCUTIO	Friend of Romeo. He is killed by Tybalt after being challenged to defend Romeo's honour.
TYBALT	Juliet's cousin. Challenges Romeo to a fight. He kills Mercutio, and then Romeo kills Tybalt.
THE NURSE	Juliet's nursemaid and confidant. Her position is compromised when she goes against Juliet's decisions about Romeo.

THEMES

Considered one of the most tragic love stories, *Romeo and Juliet* explores this idea of desire, passion and romance.

However, other key themes are also conveyed throughout the play.

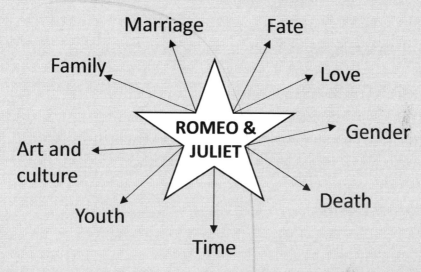

LOVE = the play deals with the romance between two young people, from families who resent one another. The whole play is based around the love that Romeo and Juliet carry for one another.

FAMILY = family is a key theme in this play. Straight from the offset, we know that the two families, the Capulets and the Montagues, are in a violent feud with one another.

DEATH = the play ends dramatically, with Romeo and Juliet both killing themselves. With Romeo thinking Juliet had killed herself, even though she had just taken a sleeping potion as part of her plan to run away, Romeo kills himself. When Juliet wakes up and finds Romeo dead, she kills herself too. Other violence is apparent including Tybalt killing Mercutio, and Romeo killing Tybalt.

YOUTH = the passion of the young lovers conflicts with their family feuds, which has a huge impact on the narrative. Romeo is about 16 years old and Juliet is about 13 years old, so this narrative shows the development of coming-of-age and romance.

EXTRACTS

*This extract is taken from **Act I Scene V.** Romeo sees Juliet for the first time.*

ROMEO
If I profane with my unworthiest hand
This holy shrine, the gentle sin is this:
My lips, two blushing pilgrims, ready stand
To smooth that rough touch with a tender kiss.
JULIET
Good pilgrim, you do wrong your hand too much,
Which mannerly devotion shows in this;
For saints have hands that pilgrims' hands do touch,
And palm to palm is holy palmers' kiss.
ROMEO
Have not saints lips, and holy palmers too?
JULIET
Ay, pilgrim, lips that they must use in prayer.
ROMEO
O, then, dear saint, let lips do what hands do;
They pray; grant thou, lest faith turn to despair.
JULIET
Saints do not move, though grant for prayers' sake.
ROMEO
Then move not, while my prayer's effect I take.
    He kisses her.
Thus from my lips, by yours, my sin is purged.
JULIET
Then have my lips the sin that they have took.
ROMEO
Sin from thy lips? O trespass sweetly urged!
Give me my sin again.
    They kiss again

*This extract is taken from **Act II Scene II**. Romeo declares his love for Juliet. (The balcony scene).*

ROMEO

He jests at scars that never felt a wound.

   Juliet appears above at a window.

But, soft! what light through yonder window breaks?

It is the east, and Juliet is the sun.

Arise, fair sun, and kill the envious moon,

Who is already sick and pale with grief,

That thou her maid art far more fair than she:

Be not her maid, since she is envious;

Her vestal livery is but sick and green

And none but fools do wear it; cast it off.

It is my lady, O, it is my love!

O, that she knew she were!

She speaks yet she says nothing: what of that?

Her eye discourses; I will answer it.

I am too bold; 'tis not to me she speaks:

Two of the fairest stars in all the heaven,

Having some business, do entreat her eyes

To twinkle in their spheres till they return.

What if her eyes were there, they in her head?

The brightness of her cheek would shame those stars,

As daylight doth a lamp; her eyes in heaven

Would through the airy region stream so bright,

That birds would sing and think it were not night.

See, how she leans her cheek upon her hand!

O, that I were a glove upon that hand,

That I might touch that cheek!

JULIET

Ay me!

ROMEO

She speaks:

O, speak again, bright angel! for thou art

As glorious to this night, being o'er my head

As is a winged messenger of heaven

Unto the white-upturned wondering eyes

Of mortals that fall back to gaze on him

When he bestrides the lazy-pacing clouds

And sails upon the bosom of the air.

JULIET

O Romeo, Romeo! wherefore art thou Romeo?

Deny thy father, and refuse thy name;

Or, if thou wilt not, be but sworn my love,

And I'll no longer be a Capulet.

ROMEO

   [Aside] Shall I hear more, or shall I speak at this?

JULIET

'Tis but thy name that is my enemy;

Thou art thyself, though not a Montague.

What's Montague? it is nor hand, nor foot,

Nor arm, nor face, nor any other part

Belonging to a man. O, be some other name!

What's in a name? that which we call a rose

By any other name would smell as sweet;

So Romeo would, were he not Romeo call'd,

Retain that dear perfection which he owes

Without that title. Romeo, doff thy name,

And for that name, which is no part of thee;

Take all myself.

This extract is taken from **Act V Scene III.** Romeo and Juliet die.

JULIET

Go, get thee hence, for I will not away.

Exit Friar Lawrence

What's here? a cup, closed in my true love's hand?

Poison, I see, hath been his timeless end:

O churl! drunk all, and left no friendly drop

To help me after? I will kiss thy lips;

Haply some poison yet doth hang on them,

To make me die with a restorative.

Kisses Romeo.

Thy lips are warm.

Enter Watchmen and Paris's Page

CHIEF WATCHMAN

(To Page) Lead, boy: which way?

JULIET

Yea, noise? then I'll be brief. O happy dagger!

Snatching Romeo's dagger

This is thy sheath; there rust, and let me die.

(Stabs herself with Romeo's dagger and dies).

PAGE

This is the place; there, where the torch doth burn.

CHIEF WATCHMAN

The ground is bloody; search about the churchyard.

Go, some of you, whoe'er you find attach.

Exeunt some Watchmen.

Pitiful sight! here lies the county slain,

And Juliet bleeding, warm, and newly dead,

Who here hath lain these two days buried.

Go, tell the prince; run to the Capulets;

Raise up the Montagues;

Some others search.

PRACTICE QUESTIONS

*For questions 1-4, refer to **Act I Scene V.***

Question 1

What imagery is conveyed throughout the passage? How does this appeal to the audience?

_____

_____

_____

_____

_____

_____

Question 2

From the opening of this passage, to when Romeo first kisses Juliet, there are 14 lines of spoken English. How does this convey poetic conventions and what does this tell the audience about their relationship?

_____

_____

_____

_____

_____

Question 3

What does "my unworthiest hand" mean? How does this tie in with family conflict?

_____

_____

_____

Question 4

What do you think Romeo and Juliet are talking about when they are discussing sins in relation to kisses?

_____

_____

_____

_____

_____

_____

*For questions 5-10, refer to **Act II Scene II.***

Question 5

What do you think Shakespeare is talking about when he uses the term "winged messenger"?

_____

_____

Question 6

Romeo talks about the moon, calling it "sick and pale with grief". What literary technique is this? Tick **one**.

Alliteration ☐

Analogy ☐

Personification ☐

Metaphor ☐

Question 7

Shakespeare contrasts day with night. What do you think this means in terms of Romeo and Juliet's relationship?

_____

_____

_____

_____

Question 8

Find a quote which highlights how Romeo compares Juliet to the stars. What does this mean in terms of his feelings for her?

_____

_____

_____

_____

Question 9

Romeo is standing in Juliet's garden. What could the garden symbolise in terms of motifs and themes?

_____

_____

_____

_____

Question 10

Why do you think Romeo is talking to Juliet from a distance, as opposed to going up to speak to her?

_____

_____

_____

_____

*For questions 11-12, refer to **Act V Scene III.***

Question 11

Shakespeare explores the theme of sacrifice. Explain the importance of this scene in terms of love.

_____

_____

_____

_____

_____

_____

Question 12

Poison plays a literal and symbolic role in the play of *Romeo and Juliet*. Romeo drinks the potion after thinking his true love is dead. Juliet's death is a consequence of the poison. Explain how the potion acts as a symbol within the narrative.

_____

_____

_____

_____

_____

_____

_____

_____

_____

_____

_____

_____

ESSAY QUESTIONS

1. Using examples from **Act II Scene II**, and other examples from *Romeo and Juliet*, how does Shakespeare explore the relationship between Romeo and Juliet? Focus on language, imagery and themes.

2. In what way does *Romeo and Juliet* break free from traditional gender conventions? Use examples from the play to support your answer.

3. Discuss how Juliet's maturity levels change from the beginning of the play to the end of the play. Why does her maturity change? What impact does this have on the audience? Why is this important to the narrative?

THE
REVISION
SERIES

MACBETH

(Analysing Plays)

MACBETH

THE STORY OF MACBETH

Macbeth is a work of tragedy and tells the story of Macbeth, a Scottish General, who is told by three witches that he will become Thane of Cawdor and King of Scotland. Although sceptical, Macbeth and his wife murder the existing king and take control of Scotland.

Following this murder, Macbeth suffers great paranoia and guilt and has to commit more murders in order to maintain his power.

The play ends with violence between Macbeth and Macduff. Macduff kills and beheads Macbeth, and Malcolm becomes the new King of Scotland.

CHARACTERS

Below I have outlined the main characters in the play, *Macbeth*.

When you read through the play, consider the following:

- *What is the purpose of each character?*
- *What role do they have in the play?*
- *How does Shakespeare want you to feel towards each character?*

MACBETH	A Scottish general who becomes Thane of Cawdor. He murders King Duncan and becomes King of Scotland. His role in the play sees him killing people in order to withhold power.
LADY MACBETH	Macbeth's wife who longs for power and position. She convinces Macbeth to murder King Duncan to become King of Scotland. She becomes riddled with guilt and commits suicide.
BANQUO	A fellow general who is told by the three witches that his children will inherit the throne. For this, Macbeth has no choice but to kill him.
DUNCAN	A well-respected and honoured King of Scotland. He decides to pass on the throne to his son, Malcolm. Macbeth kills him.
MACDUFF	A nobleman who discovers Duncan's death. Macduff joins Malcolm in England, but wants revenge when Macbeth threatens the death of his family.
DONALBAIN AND MALCOLM	The sons of King Duncan. They flee the country thinking whoever killed their father would be after them. Donalbain flees to Ireland and Malcom flees to England. Malcolm decides to raise an army in hope to bring down the tyrant Macbeth.

THEMES

Macbeth contains several themes.

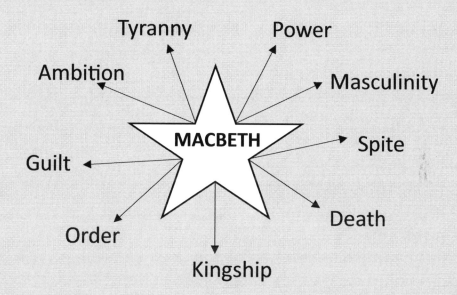

MASCULINITY = there are clear issues surrounding gender roles. Lady Macbeth has a huge influence over her husband, and is able to manipulate him into killing King Duncan. Both Macbeth and Lady Macbeth demonstrate their negative character by provoking the murderers they hire to kill the others.

TYRANNY = although Macbeth exceeds to the throne, he is not worshipped as a king. Instead, he is known as a "tyrant" – someone who is a cruel and oppressive ruler. The power Macbeth has is uncontrollable; and he is unable to control his ambition and authority, which is clearly demonstrated by his inability to rule with honour and harmony.

GUILT = the theme of guilt is clearly conveyed in the play, *Macbeth*. Lady Macbeth shows clear guilt and remorse, which becomes so bad, she commits suicide. The hallucinations which she and Macbeth both suffer indicates their feelings of guilt.

AMBITION = ambition is a key theme in this play, as the actions of Macbeth and Lady Macbeth are based on their ambitions to gain power and the throne.

EXTRACTS

This extract is taken from **Act I Scene VII.** *Lady Macbeth and Macbeth discuss their plan to kill King Duncan.*

MACBETH

If we should fail?

LADY MACBETH

We fail!

But screw your courage to the sticking-place,

And we'll not fail. When Duncan is asleep –

Whereto the rather shall his day's hard journey

Soundly invite him – his two chamberlains

Will I with wine and wassail so convince

That memory, the warder of the brain,

Shall be a fume, and the receipt of reason

A limbeck only: when in swinish sleep

Their drenched natures lie as in a death,

What cannot you and I perform upon

The unguarded Duncan? what not put upon

His spongy officers, who shall bear the guilt

Of our great quell?

MACBETH

Bring forth men-children only;

For thy undaunted mettle should compose

Nothing but males. Will it not be received,

When we have mark'd with blood those sleepy two

Of his own chamber and used their very daggers,

That they have done't?

LADY MACBETH

Who dares receive it other,

As we shall make our griefs and clamour roar

Upon his death?

MACBETH

I am settled, and bend up

Each corporal agent to this terrible feat.

Away, and mock the time with fairest show:

False face must hide what the false heart doth know.

Exeunt

*This extract is taken from **Act V Scene I.** A doctor and gentlewoman watch Lady Macbeth sleepwalking.*

> *Enter Lady Macbeth with a taper*
>
> Lo you, here she comes! This is her very guise; and, upon my life, fast asleep. Observe her; stand close.
>
> **DOCTOR**
>
> How came she by that light?
>
> **GENTLEWOMAN**
>
> Why, it stood by her: she has light by her continually; 'tis her command.
>
> **DOCTOR**
>
> You see, her eyes are open.
>
> **GENTLEWOMAN**
>
> Ay, but their sense is shut.
>
> **DOCTOR**
>
> What is it she does now? Look, how she rubs her hands.
>
> **GENTLEWOMAN**
>
> It is an accustomed action with her, to seem thus washing her hands: I have known her continue in this a quarter of an hour.
>
> **LADY MACBETH**
>
> Yet here's a spot.
>
> **DOCTOR**
>
> Hark! she speaks: I will set down what comes from her, to satisfy my remembrance the more strongly.
>
> **LADY MACBETH**
>
> Out, damned spot! out, I say! – One, two: why, then, 'tis time to do't. Hell is murky! Fie, my lord, fie! a soldier, and afeard? What need we fear who knows it, when none can call our power to account? – Yet who would have thought the old man to have had so much blood in him.
>
> **DOCTOR**
>
> Do you mark that?
>
> **LADY MACBETH**
>
> The thane of Fife had a wife: where is she now? – What, will these hands

ne'er be clean? – No more o' that, my lord, no more o' that: you mar all with this starting.

DOCTOR

Go to, go to; you have known what you should not.

GENTLEWOMAN

She has spoke what she should not, I am sure of that: heaven knows what she has known.

LADY MACBETH

Here's the smell of the blood still: all the perfumes of Arabia will not sweeten this little hand. Oh, Oh, Oh!

DOCTOR

What a sigh is there! The heart is sorely charged.

GENTLEWOMAN

I would not have such a heart in my bosom for the dignity of the whole body.

DOCTOR

Well, well, well.

GENTLEWOMAN

Play God it be, sir.

DOCTOR

This disease is beyond my practice: yet I have known those which have walked in their sleep who have died holily in their beds.

LADY MACBETH

Wash your hands, put on your nightgown; look not so pale. – I tell you yet again, Banquo's buried; he cannot come out on's grave.

DOCTOR

Even so?

LADY MACBETH

To bed, to bed; there's knocking at the gate: come, come, come, come, give me your hand. What's done cannot be undone. – To bed, to bed, to bed!

Exit

*This extract is taken from **Act V Scene VIII**. Macbeth is killed.*

Enter Macduff with Macbeth's head.

MACDUFF

Hail, king! for so thou art: behold, where stands

The usurper's cursed head: the time is free:

I see thee compass'd with thy kingdom's pearl,

That speak my salutation in their minds;

Whose voices I desire aloud with mine.

Hail, King of Scotland!

ALL

Hail, King of Scotland!

Flourish

MALCOLM

We shall not spend a large expense of time

Before we reckon with your several loves,

And make us even with you. My thanes and kinsmen,

Henceforth be earls, the first that ever Scotland

In such an honour named. What's more to do,

Which would be planted newly with the time,

As calling home our exiled friends abroad,

That fled the snares of watchful tyranny;

Producing forth the cruel ministers

Of this dead butcher and his fiend-like queen,

Who, as 'tis thought, by self and violent hands

Took off her life; this, and what needful else

That calls upon us, by the grace of Grace,

We will perform in measure, time, and place.

So, thanks to all at once and to each one,

Whom we invite to see us crown'd at Scone.

Flourish. Exeunt.

PRACTICE QUESTIONS

*For questions 1-4, refer to **Act I Scene VII.***

Question 1

"False face must hide what the false heart doth know."

How does this line of Macbeth's speech convey the theme of appearance vs. reality?

_____

_____

_____

_____

_____

_____

Question 2

Describe how Lady Macbeth's speech demonstrates issues related to gender roles.

_____

_____

_____

_____

_____

_____

_____

Question 3

"Bring forth men-children only; / For thy undaunted mettle should compose / Nothing but males."

Shakespeare explores the importance of masculinity throughout the play of *Macbeth*. Using the example above, explain how Shakespeare is challenging a misogynistic culture.

How is this relevant to the time in which the play was written? What impact would this have on the audience?

_____

_____

_____

_____

_____

_____

_____

_____

Question 4

"I am settled, and bend up / Each corporal agent to this terrible feat."

What does this line mean? Explain the influence of Lady Macbeth's character on her husband.

_____

_____

_____

_____

_____

For questions 5-8, refer to *Act V Scene I.*

Question 5

In Act V Scene I, Lady Macbeth makes constant references to "blood". Explain how the blood acts a symbol for her guilty conscience.

_____

_____

_____

_____

_____

Question 6

Describe how Lady Macbeth's sleepwalking is a sign of physical decline in her strength and power.

_____

_____

_____

_____

_____

Question 7

What themes are conveyed in this extract? How do they relate to the overall narrative?

_____

_____

_____

_____

_____

Question 8

What senses are addressed in the extract? What does this say to the audience about the role of Lady Macbeth?

_____

_____

_____

_____

_____

_____

_____

*For questions 9-12, refer to **Act V Scene VIII.***

Question 9

The stage direction *"Enter Macduff with Macbeth's head"* shows the visual defeat of Macbeth's character. Why do you think Shakespeare shows this to his audience?

_____

_____

_____

_____

_____

_____

Question 10

In Macbeth's speech, he refers to Macbeth as a "tyrant". What do you think this means? Explain the importance this has on how he is perceived by both the audience and other characters.

_____

_____

_____

_____

_____

_____

Question 11

How does this final Act explore the theme of Kingship vs. tyranny?

_____

_____

_____

_____

_____

_____

_____

_____

_____

_____

_____

Question 12

Using this extract, and knowledge about the play, show whether you agree or disagree with the following statement: "The play of *Macbeth* is based on evil and defeat".

_____

_____

_____

_____

_____

_____

_____

_____

_____

_____

_____

_____

ESSAY QUESTIONS

1. How much is Macbeth the victim of his own fate? How does his character spiral downwards as the play progresses?

2. Discuss the influence of the witches' prophecies and how this stirs the action that occurs in the play.

3. Explore the nature of the supernatural. Pay attention to key ideas including hallucinations and ghosts, the role of the witches and the floating dagger. Why is the theme of the supernatural important to the tragic story of *Macbeth*?

THE
REVISION
SERIES

AS YOU LIKE IT

(Analysing Plays)

AS YOU LIKE IT

THE STORY OF AS YOU LIKE IT

A pastoral comedy which sees the brewing romance between Rosalind and Orlando. *As You Like It* is a play that deals with banishment, gender role reversals, romance, cross-dressing, marriage and religion.

CHARACTERS

Below I have outlined the main characters in the play, *As You Like It*.

When you read through the play, consider the following:

- *What is the purpose of each character?*
- *What role do they have in the play?*
- *How does Shakespeare want you to feel towards each character?*

ROSALIND	Daughter of banished Duke Senior. She falls in love with Orlando. When she leaves the court and enters the forest, she dresses up as a man.
ORLANDO	Youngest son of Sir Rowland de Bois and brother to Oliver. He is victorious in his battle against Charles, and saves his brother's life (despite his brother being less than pleasant to him).
JAQUES	He is a by-stander to most of the action that takes place between the characters.
OLIVER	Oldest son of Sir Rowland de Bois and brother to Orlando. He admits to hating his brother, and goes to great lengths to destroy him. His character transforms as the play escalates, and falls in love for the disguised Celia.
CELIA	Rosalind's cousin and close friend. They both travel to the Forest of Arden. She goes to the forest disguised as Aliena. She falls in love with Oliver.
TOUCHSTONE	Court clown. Accompanies Celia and Rosalind to the Forest of Arden. He falls in love with Audrey.

AS YOU LIKE IT

THEMES

As You Like It contains several themes.

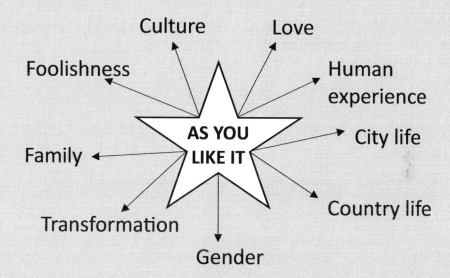

FAMILY = Shakespeare explores the idea of family. The relationships within this play illustrate another key theme of loyalty/disloyalty. We see this a number of times throughout the play, with the characters Oliver and Orlando, Celia and Rosalind, Celia and Duke Fredrick and many others.

LOVE = the idea of love and desire is apparent throughout the narrative. Same-sex desire is also touched upon with the characters of Phoebe and Rosalind, Rosalind and Celia, and "Ganymede" and Orlando.

CONTRASTS BETWEEN CITY AND COUNTRY LIFE = the play explores both city life and country life which is apparent across much of pastoral literature. Shakespeare compares the French courts with the Forest of Arden.

TRANSFORMATION = the Forest of Arden is where most of the transformations take place. The audience view the art of cross-dressing and psychological and spiritual changes, which suggest that humans are adaptable and able to change their ways.

EXTRACTS

*This extract is taken from **Act II Scene I.** Duke Senior is discussing the wonders of the forest.*

DUKE SENIOR

Now, my co-mates and brothers in exile,

Hath not old custom made this life more sweet

Than that of painted pomp? Are not these woods

More free from peril than the envious court?

Here feel we but the penalty of Adam,

The seasons' difference, as the icy fang

And churlish chiding of the winter's wind,

Which, when it bites and blows upon my body,

Even till I shrink with cold, I smile and say

'This is no flattery; these are counsellors

That feelingly persuade me what I am.'

Sweet are the uses of adversity,

Which, like the toad, ugly and venomous,

Wears yet a precious jewel in his head.

And this our life, exempt from public haunt,

Find tongues in trees, books in the running brooks,

Sermons in stones, and good in everything.

I would not change it.

AMIENS

Happy is your Grace,

That can translate the stubbornness of fortune

Into so quiet and so sweet a style.

DUKE SENIOR

Come, shall we go and kill us venison?

And yet it irks me the poor dappled fools,

Being native burghers of this desert city,

Should in their own confines with forked heads

Have their round haunches gored.

*This extract is taken from **Act II Scene III**. Adam is telling Orlando that he should not return home because of his brother, Oliver.*

ORLANDO

Why, whither, Adam, wouldst thou have me go?

ADAM

No matter whither, so you come not here.

ORLANDO

What, wouldst thou have me go and beg my food?

Or with a base and boisterous sword enforce

A thievish living on the common road?

This I must do, or know not what to do:

Yet this I will not do, do how I can;

I rather will subject me to the malice

Of a diverted blood and bloody brother.

ADAM

But do not so. I have five hundred crowns,

The thrifty hire I saved under your father,

Which I did store to be my foster-nurse

When service should in my old limbs lie lame

And unregarded age in corners thrown:

Take that, and He that doth the ravens feed,

Yea, providently caters for the sparrow,

Be comfort to my age! Here is the gold;

And all this I give you. Let me be your servant:

Though I look old, yet I am strong and lusty;

For in my youth I never did apply

Hot and rebellious liquors in my blood,

Nor did not with unbashful forehead woo

The means of weakness and debility;

Therefore my age is as a lusty winter,

Frosty, but kindly: let me go with you;

I'll do the service of a younger man
In all your business and necessities.
ORLANDO
O good old man, how well in thee appears
The constant service of the antique world,
When service sweat for duty, not for meed!
Thou art not for the fashion of these times,
Where none will sweat but for promotion,
And having that, do choke their service up
Even with the having: it is not so with thee.
But, poor old man, thou prunest a rotten tree,
That cannot so much as a blossom yield
In lieu of all thy pains and husbandry.
But come thy ways: we'll go along together,
And ere we have thy youthful wages spent,
We'll light upon some settled low content.
ADAM
Master, go on, and I will follow thee,
To the last gasp, with truth and loyalty.
From seventeen years till now almost fourscore
Here lived I, but now live here no more.
At seventeen years many their fortunes seek;
But as fourscore it is too late a week:
Yet fortune cannot recompense me better
Than to die well and not my master's debtor.
  Exit.

*This extract is taken from **Act V Scene IV**. Rosalind's epilogue.*

Exeunt all but Rosalind.

ROSALIND

It is not the fashion to see the lady the epilogue;
but it is no more unhandsome than to see the lord
the prologue. If it be true that good wine needs no
bush, 'tis true that a good play needs no epilogue:
yet to good wine they do use good bushes, and
good plays prove the better by the help of good
epilogues. What a case am I in, then, that am
neither a good epilogue, nor cannot insinuate with
you in the behalf of a good play. I am not furnished
like a beggar, therefore to beg will not become
me. My way is to conjure you, and I'll begin with
the women. I charge you, O women, for the love
you bear to men, to like as much of this play as
please you: and I charge you, O men, for the love
you bear to women – as I perceive by your simpering,
none of you hates them –, that between you
and the women the play may please. If I were a woman,
I would kiss as many of you as had beards that pleased
me, complexions that liked me, and breaths that I defied
not: and, I am sure, as many as have good beards,
or good faces, or sweet breaths will, for my kind offer,
when I make curtsy, bid me farewell.

Exeunt

PRACTICE QUESTIONS

*For questions 1-4, refer to **Act II Scene I.***

Question 1

Shakespeare uses figurative language throughout the play of *As You Like It*.

Find two examples of alliteration and explain the effect this literary technique has on the audience.

ALLITERATION 1

ALLITERATION 2

EFFECT

Question 2

How does the speech from Duke Senior explore this idea of pastoral imagery? Why does Shakespeare explore the notion of pastoral imagery?

Question 3

> *"Here feel we but the penalty of Adam,*
> *The seasons' difference, as the icy fang*
> *And churlish chiding of the winter's wind,*
> *Which, when it bites and blows upon my body,*
> *Even till I shrink with cold, I smile and say,*
> *'This is no flattery; these are counsellors*
> *That feelingly persuade me what I am.'"*

What is this saying? How is this ironic to the overall theme of the narrative?

_____

_____

_____

_____

_____

_____

_____

Question 4

> *"Find tongues in trees, books in the running brooks, / Sermons in stones, and good in everything".*

What does this sentence mean and what does it say to the audience about Duke Senior?

_____

_____

_____

_____

_____

_____

---

*For questions 5-8, refer to **Act II Scene III**.*

Question 5

"I rather will subject me to the malice / Of a diverted blood and bloody brother."

How does this line represent the relationship between Orlando and his brother Oliver?

_____

_____

_____

_____

_____

_____

Question 6

"O good old man, how well in thee appears / The constant service of the antique world, / When service sweat for duty, not for meed! / Thou art not for the fashion of these times."

Compare and contrast the views of Shakespeare's language to views of modern day society.

_____

_____

_____

_____

_____

_____

Question 7

Describe the relationship between Orlando and Adam.

_____

_____

_____

_____

_____

_____

_____

_____

_____

Question 8

In Adam's speech, beginning with *"Master, go on, and I will follow thee"*, Shakespeare uses verses to emphasise the character as being noble.

Using examples from this extract, explain the importance of Shakespeare's language and how the rhyming pattern creates a powerful image.

_____

_____

_____

_____

_____

_____

_____

_____

_____

For questions 9-12, refer to *Act V Scene IV.*

Question 9

Why do you think Shakespeare ends the play, *As You Like It,* with an epilogue from Rosalind?

_____

_____

_____

_____

_____

_____

_____

_____

Question 10

> *"It is not the fashion to see the lady the epilogue but it is no more unhandsome than to see the lord the prologue."*

Throughout the play, Rosalind pretends to be a man pretending to be a woman. How is Rosalind's epilogue the perfect fit to end the play?

_____

_____

_____

_____

_____

_____

_____

Question 11

"I am not furnished like a beggar; therefore to beg will not become me."

What does Rosalind mean by this line?

_____

_____

_____

_____

_____

_____

Question 12

When Rosalind addresses the men in the audience, she states *"If I were a woman, I would kiss as many of you."*

Explain how this line suggests that the character of Rosalind is played by a man? Why is this relevant to Shakespearean times?

_____

_____

_____

_____

_____

_____

_____

_____

_____

_____

_____

ESSAY QUESTIONS

1. Discuss the theme of family in *As You Like It*. Support your answer using two or more characters to strengthen your answer.

2. How is Orlando and Rosalind's relationship portrayed? Consider the use of language and imagery.

3. How does Shakespeare use language to emphasise class differences between the characters? Why is this important to Shakespearean audiences?

THE
REVISION
SERIES

THE TAMING
OF THE SHREW

(Analysing Plays)

THE TAMING OF THE SHREW

THE STORY OF THE TAMING OF THE SHREW

The Taming of the Shrew is another comedy of Shakespeare. The main plot of this play is the courtship between Katherina (the bad-tempered and resentful daughter) and Petruchio (a character in search of the 'right' wife).

Their relationship begins with Katherina being very unwilling and headstrong, but Petruchio soon 'tames' the 'shrew', and makes her a compliant wife.

Another plotline in this play includes Bianca's suitors and their attempts to 'woo' her. Her father Baptista refuses to let Bianca marry before his eldest daughter.

CHARACTERS

Below I have outlined the main characters in the play, *The Taming of the Shrew*.

When you read through the play, consider the following:

- *What is the purpose of each character?*
- *What role do they have in the play?*
- *How does Shakespeare want you to feel towards each character?*

KATHERINA	A strong-minded and independent woman who doesn't like to be held down by others. She is courted by Petruchio, who attempts to make her a compliant bride.

PETRUCHIO	Petruchio is in the hunt for a bride, and when he hears about Katherina's feistiness, he attempts to woo her.

BIANCA	Katherina's younger sister, who has many male suitors.

BAPTISTA	The father of Katherina and Bianca. He is a wealthy citizen in Padua, and wants to find suitable husbands for both his daughters. However, he refuses to allow Bianca to marry before Katherina.

THE SUITORS	Gremio, Hortensio and Lucentio are all male suitors for Bianca. Lucencio falls in love with Bianca.

THEMES

Below I have outlined the key themes in *The Taming of the Shrew*.

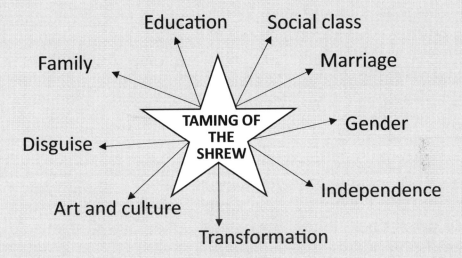

MARRIAGE = the play focuses on marriage and mocks the power struggles between male and female roles. Although the play does focus on 16th century matrimonial values, it also uses language that suggests quite perverse attitudes.

FAMILY AND RELATIONSHIPS = the theme of family is apparent throughout the play. Not only do we have the main relationship of Katherina and Petruchio, but we also see relationships created with Bianca and her suitors, and the family bond between Baptista, Katherina and Bianca.

TRANSFORMATION = one of the biggest transformations we see is through the character of Katherina. Early on in the play, Katherina is described as being bad-tempered, independent and challenging. She has a male suitor, Petruchio, who attempts to 'woo' her. He attempts to deal with her challenging behaviour until she eventually caves in and marries him.

EXTRACTS

*This extract is taken from **Act II Scene I.** Petruchio is talking about wooing Katherina.*

> *Exeunt all but Petruchio.*
> And woo her with some spirit when she comes,
> Say that she rail; why then I'll tell her plain,
> She sings as sweetly as a nightingale:
> Say that she frown; I'll say she looks as clear
> As morning roses newly wash'd with dew:
> Say she be mute and will not speak a word;
> Then I'll commend her volubility,
> And say she uttereth piercing eloquence:
> If she do bid me pack, I'll give her thanks,
> As though she bid me stay by her a week:
> If she deny to wed, I'll crave the day
> When I shall ask the banns, and when be married.
> But here she comes, and now, Petruchio, speak.
> *Enter Katherina*
> Good morrow, Kate; for that's your name, I hear.
> **KATHERINA**
> Well have you heard, but something hard of hearing:
> They call me Katherina that do talk of me.
> **PETRUCHIO**
> You lie, in faith; for you are call'd plain Kate,
> And bonny Kate, and sometimes Kate the curst;
> But Kate, the prettiest Kate in Christendom,
> Kate of Kate-Hall, my super-dainty Kate,
> For dainties are all Kates, and therefore, Kate,
> Take this of me, Kate of me consolation;
> Hearing thy mildness praised in every town,
> Thy virtues spoke of, and thy beauty sounded,
> Yet not so deeply as to thee belongs,
> Myself am moved to woo thee for my wife.

*This extract is taken from **Act III Scene II**. Petruchio's wedding costume.*

BIONDELLO

Why, Petruchio is coming in a new hat and an old jerkin; a pair of old breeches thrice turned; a pair of boots that have been candle-cases, one buckled, another laced; an old rusty sword ta'en out of the town armoury, with a broken hilt, and chapeless; with two broken points: his horse hipped with an old mothy saddle and stirrups of no kindred; besides, possess'd with the glanders, and like to mose in the chine; troubled with the lampass, infected with the fashions, full of windgalls, sped with spavins, ray'd with the yellows, past cure of the fives, stark spoiled with the staggers, begnawn with the bots, sway'd in the back, and shoulder-shotten; near-legg'd before, and with a half-cheek'd bit, and a headstall of sheep's leather, which, being restrain'd to keep him from stumbling, hath been often burst and now repair'd with knots; one girth six times pieced, and a woman's crupper of velure, which hath two letters for her name fairly set down in studs, and here and there pieced with packthread.

BAPTISTA

Who comes with him?

BIONDELLO

O, sir, his lackey, for all the world caparison'd like the horse; with a linen stock on one leg and a kersey boot-hose on the other, garter'd with a red and blue list; an old hat, and *The Humour of Forty Fancies* prick'd in't for a feather: a monster, a very monster in apparel, and not like a Christian footboy or a gentleman's lackey.

TRANIO

'Tis some odd humour pricks him to this fashion,
Yet oftentimes he goes but mean-apparell'd.

BAPTISTA

I am glad he's come, howsoe'ver he comes.

BIONDELLO

Why, sir, he comes not.

BAPTISTA

Didst thou not say he comes?

BIONDELLO

Who? that Petruchio came?

BAPTISTA

Ay, that Petruchio came.

BIONDELLO

No, sir, I say his horse comes, with him on his back.

BAPTISTA

Why, that's all one.

BIONDELLO

Nay, by Saint Jamy.

I hold you a penny,

A horse and a man

Is more than one,

And yet not many.

    Enter Petruchio and Grumio

PETRUCHIO

Come, where be these gallants? who's at home?

BAPTISTA

You are welcome, sir.

PETRUCHIO

And yet I come not well.

BAPTISTA

And yet you halt not.

TRANIO

Not so well apparell'd

As I wish you were.

PETRUCHIO

Were it better, I should rush in thus.

But where is Kate? where is my lovely bride?

How does my father? Gentles, methinks you frown:

And wherefore gaze this goodly company,

As if they saw some wondrous monument,

Some comet or unusual prodigy?

*This extract is taken from **Act V Scene II**. Katherina expressing her feelings.*

KATHERINA
Fie, fie! unknit that threatening unkind brow,
And dart not scornful glances from those eyes,
To wound thy lord, thy king, thy governor:
It blots thy beauty, as frosts do bite the meads;
Confounds thy fame, as whirlwinds shake fair buds;
And in no sense is meet or amiable.
A woman mov'd is like a fountain troubled,
Muddy, ill-seeming, thick, bereft of beauty;
And while it is so, none so dry or thirsty
Will deign to sip, or touch one drop of it.
Thy husband is thy lord, thy life, thy keeper,
Thy head, thy sovereign; one that cares for thee,
And for thy maintenance commits his body
To painful labour both by sea and land,
To watch the night in storms, the day in cold,
Whilst thou liest warm at home, secure and safe;
And craves no other tribute at thy hands
But love, fair looks, and true obedience, –
Too little payment for so great a debt.
Such duty as a the subject owes the prince,
Even such a woman oweth to her husband;
And when she is froward, peevish, sullen, sour,
And not obedient to his honest will,
What is she but a foul contending rebel,
And graceless traitor to her loving lord?
I am asham'd that women are so simple
To offer war where they should kneel for peace;
Or seek for rule, supremacy, and sway,
When they are bound to serve, love, and obey.
Why are our bodies soft and weak and smooth,

Unapt to toil and trouble in the world,
But that our soft conditions and our hearts
Should well agree with our external parts?
Come, come, you froward and unable worms!
My mind hath been as big as one of yours,
My heart as great, my reason haply more,
To bandy word for word and frown for frown:
But now I see our lances are but straws,
Our strength as weak, our weakness past compare,
That seeming to be most, which we indeed least are.
Then vail your stomachs, for it is no boot,
And place your hands below your husband's foot:
In token of which duty, if he please,
My hand is ready, may it do him ease.

PRACTICE QUESTIONS

*For questions 1-4, refer to **Act II Scene I.***

Question 1

Why do you think Petruchio repeats Kate's name several times?

_____

_____

_____

_____

_____

_____

Question 2

Discuss how Petruchio's attempt to woo Katherina is by counteracting everything she says and does. What does this say about gender roles?

_____

_____

_____

_____

_____

_____

_____

_____

Question 3

When Katherina enters, Petruchio greets her as "Kate". However, Katherina adamantly corrects him and states that everyone calls her "Katherina".

Why do you think Petruchio continues to address her as "Kate"?

_____

_____

_____

_____

_____

_____

_____

_____

_____

Question 4

Describe the power struggles between Katherina and Petruchio.

_____

_____

_____

_____

_____

_____

_____

_____

_____

*For questions 5-8, refer to **Act III Scene II.***

Question 5

What does Petruchio's ridiculous wedding attire symbolise? What does this suggest to the audience?

_____

_____

_____

_____

_____

_____

_____

_____

_____

Question 6

"Not so well apparell'd / As I wish you were."

What does this say about the way Petruchio is dressed? Why do you think Tranio has this response to Petruchio's old clothing?

_____

_____

_____

_____

_____

_____

_____

Question 7

"I am glad he's come, howsoe'er he comes"

Baptista is implying that he was unsure whether Petruchio would go through with marrying his "shrew" of a daughter.

Agree or disagree: Baptista would go to any lengths to find his daughter a husband. How does this fit in with a Shakespearean audience?

Question 8

"But where is Kate? where is my lovely bride? / How does my father? Gentles, methinks you frown: / And wherefore gaze this goodly company, / As if they saw some wondrous monument, / Some comet or unusual prodigy?"

Analyse Petruchio's feelings towards his future bride. What do you think Petruchio is referring to by *"some comet or unusual prodigy"*?

For questions 9-12, refer to *Act V Scene II.*

Question 9

Shakespeare uses figurative language in Katherina's speech to speak about gender roles.

Find two similes in this extract, and explain what Shakespeare is trying to say.

SIMILE 1

_____

EXPLANATION

_____

_____

_____

SIMILE 2

_____

EXPLANATION

_____

_____

_____

Question 10

"Why are our bodies soft and weak and smooth, / Unapt to toil and trouble in the world, / But that our soft conditions and our hearts / Should well agree with our external parts?"

What does this say about women in general, in contrast to the male roles?

_____

_____

_____

_____

_____

_____

_____

_____

_____

_____

Question 11

Agree or disagree: Katherina's representation in this final Act emphasises how she is now "tamed"?

_____

_____

_____

_____

_____

_____

_____

_____

_____

Question 12

Using examples from the extract, explore how Shakespeare presents the motif of domestication.

_____

_____

_____

_____

_____

_____

_____

_____

_____

_____

_____

_____

ESSAY QUESTIONS

1. Compare and contrast the theme of reality vs. appearance in *The Taming of the Shrew*.

2. Explore the main criticism that Shakespeare represents women as being "objects". To what extent of this is true? Why do you think Shakespeare chooses to represent his female characters in this way?

3. Compare and contrast the two sisters, *Katherina and Bianca*, using examples from both the beginning of the play and the end of the play. What do you learn from each character and why is this important to the overall narrative of *The Taming of the Shrew?*

THE
REVISION
SERIES

A MIDSUMMER NIGHT'S DREAM

(Analysing Plays)

A MIDSUMMER NIGHT'S DREAM

THE STORY OF A MIDSUMMER NIGHT'S DREAM

A Midsummer Night's Dream is a comedy, which is considered one of Shakespeare's most popular plays.

The play is based on the marriage of Theseus and Hippolyta. They experience adventures alongside other characters in the forest – the place where most of the play is set.

Forest fairies control and manipulate the characters, which bring elements of fantasy and adventure to a play of romance and marriage.

CHARACTERS

Below I have outlined the main characters in the play, *A Midsummer Night's Dream.*

When you read through the play, consider the following:

- *What is the purpose of each character?*
- *What role do they have in the play?*
- *How does Shakespeare want you to feel towards each character?*

THESEUS	Duke of Athens and hero of Greek mythology. Won a war against the Amazons. He intends to marry Hippolyta.
HIPPOLYTA	Queen of the Amazons. She is betrothed to Theseus, after his win against the Amazons.
HERMIA	Egeus's daughter. She has male suitors (Demetrius and Lysander). Her father wants her to marry Demetrius, but she has fallen in love with Lysander.
NICK BOTTOM	Overconfident weaver. He plays Pyramus in the play for Theseus's marital celebrations.
PUCK	"Robin Goodfellow". Mischievous fairy who likes playing pranks on mortals.
HELENA	A woman in love with Demetrius, even though he has rejected her. She is a self-pitiful character who runs into danger.
TITANIA	Queen of the fairies.

A MIDSUMMER NIGHT'S DREAM

THEMES

Below I have outlined the key themes in A Midsummer Night's Dream.

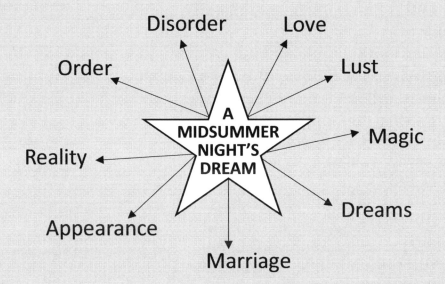

LOVE = love is one of the major themes in A Midsummer Night's Dream. Shakespeare explores the theme of love through a range of characters, with huge focus on Theseus and Hippolyta. Other examples of this idea include: Hermia and Lysander, Helena's love for Demetrius and Demetrius's love for Hermia.

Shakespeare often explores love with this idea of beauty.

MAGIC = magic is used to create the image of surrealism and supernatural powers. The fairies use their magic in order to create events that appear bizarre and comical.

DREAMS = dream-like qualities are often conveyed throughout A Midsummer Night's Dream. This is closely linked to the magic that occurs in the forest. Characters often talk about their dreams and try to recall events that have happened that seem bizarre to them.

EXTRACTS

*This extract is taken from **Act I Scene I.** Theseus and Hippolyta are discussing their wedding.*

> *Enter Theseus, Hippolyta, and Philostrate with others.*
> **THESEUS**
> Now, fair Hippolyta, our nuptial hour
> Draws on apace; four happy days bring in
> Another moon: but, O, methinks how slow
> This old moon wanes! she lingers my desires,
> Like to a step-dame, or a dowager,
> Long withering out a young man's revenue.
> **HIPPOLYTA**
> Four days will quickly steep themselves in night;
> Four nights will quickly dream away the time;
> And then the moon, like to a silver bow
> New-bent in heaven, shall behold the night
> Of our solemnities.
> **THESEUS**
> Go, Philostrate,
> Stir up the Athenian youth to merriments;
> Awake the pert and nimble spirit of mirth:
> Turn melancholy forth to funerals,
> The pale companion is not for our pomp.
> *Exit Philostrate.*
> Hippolyta, I woo'd thee with my sword,
> And won thy love, doing thee injuries;
> But I will wed thee in another key,
> With pomp, with triumph, and with revelling.
> *Enter Egeus and his daughter Hermia, and Lysander and Demetrius.*
> **EGEUS**
> Happy be Theseus, our renowned duke!
> **THESEUS**
> Thanks, good Egeus: what's the news with thee?

EGEUS

Full of vexation come I, with complaint
Against my child, my daughter Hermia.
Stand forth, Demetrius. My noble lord,
This man hath my consent to marry her.
Stand forth, Lysander. And my gracious duke,
This man hath bewitch'd the bosom of my child. –
Thou, thou, Lysander, thou hast given her rhymes,
And interchanged love-tokens with my child:
Thou hast by moonlight at her window sung,
With feigning voice verses of feigning love,
And stol'n the impression of her fantasy
With bracelets of thy hair, rings, gawds, conceits,
Knacks, trifles, nosegays, sweetmeats, – messengers
Of strong prevailment in unharden'd youth:
With cunning hast thou filch'd my daughter's heart;
Turn'd her obedience, which is due to me,
To stubborn harshness: and, my gracious duke,
Be it so she will not here before your grace
Consent to marry with Demetrius,
I beg the ancient privilege of Athens,
As she is mine, I may dispose of her:
Which shall be either to this gentleman
Or to her death, according to our law
Immediately provided in that case.

*This extract is taken from **Act II Scene I.** Introducing the King and Queen of the fairy realm.*

TITANIA
What, jealous Oberon! – Fairies, skip hence:
I have forsworn his bed and company.
OBERON
Tarry, rash wanton: am not I thy lord?
TITANIA
Then I must be thy lady: but I know
When thou hast stol'n away from fairy-land,
And in the shape of Corin sat all day,
Playing on pipes of corn and versing love
To amorous Phillida. Why art thou here,
Come from the farthest steep of India?
But that, forsooth, the bouncing Amazon,
Your buskin'd mistress and your warrior love,
To Theseus must be wedded, and you come
To give their bed joy and prosperity.
OBERON
How canst thou thus for shame, Titania,
Glance at my credit with Hippolyta,
Knowing I know thy love to Theseus?
Didst thou not lead him through the glimmering night
From Perigenia, whom he ravished?
And make him with fair Aegles break his faith,
With Ariadne and Antiopa?
TITANIA
These are the forgeries of jealousy:
And never, since the middle summer's spring,
Met we on hill, in dale, forest, or mead,
By paved fountain or by rushy brook,
Or in the beached margent of the sea,

To dance our ringlets to the whistling wind,
But with thy brawls thou hast disturb'd our sport.
Therefore the winds, piping to us in vain,
As in revenge, have suck'd up from the sea
Contagious fogs; which falling in the land,
Have every pelting river made so proud
That they have overborne their continents:
The ox hath therefore stretch'd his yoke in vain,
The ploughman lost his sweat, and the green corn
Hath rotted ere his youth attain'd a beard:
The fold stands empty in the drowned field,
And crows are fatted with the murrion flock.
The nine-men's-morris is fill'd up with mud,
And the quaint mazes in the wanton green
For lack of tread are undistinguishable:
The human mortals want their winter here.
No night is now with hymn or carol blest:
Therefore the moon, the governess of floods,
Pale in her anger, washes all the air,
That rheumatic diseases do abound.
And thorough this distemperature we see
The seasons alter: hoary-headed frosts
Fall in the fresh lap of the crimson rose,
And on old Hiem's thin and icy crown
An odorous chaplet of sweet summer buds
Is, as in mockery, set: the spring, the summer,
The childing autumn, angry winter, change
Their wonted liveries, and the mazed world,
By their increase, now knows not which is which:
And this same progeny of evil comes
From our debate, from our dissension;
We are their parents and original.

*This extract is taken from **Act V Scene I**. Robin addresses the audience with this last speech.*

> *Exeunt all but Robin.*
>
> **ROBIN**
>
> If we shadows have offended,
> Think but this, and all is mended, –
> That you have but slumber'd here
> While these visions did appear.
> And this weak and idle theme,
> No more yielding but a dream,
> Gentles, do not reprehend:
> If you pardon, we will mend.
> And, as I am an honest Puck,
> If we have unearned luck
> Now to 'scape the serpent's tongue,
> We will make amends ere long;
> Else the Puck a liar call:
> So, good night unto you all.
> Give me your hands, if we be friends,
> And Robin shall restore amends.
>
> *Exit.*

PRACTICE QUESTIONS

For questions 1-4, refer to **Act I Scene I.**

Question 1

> "Now, fair Hippolyta, our nuptial hour
> Draws on apace. Four happy days bring in
> Another moon. But O, methinks how slow
> This old moon wanes! she lingers my desires,
> Like to a step-dame or a dowager
> Long withering out a young man's revenue."

What imagery is created in this extract and why is it relevant?

_____

_____

_____

_____

_____

_____

Question 2

Find a quote from the passage showing this idea of arranged marriage. What does this say about marriage in Shakespearean times?

_____

_____

_____

_____

_____

_____

Question 3

Using the characters of Egeus and Hermia, Shakespeare draws upon the idea that women are subject to a male figure – whether that figure is a father or husband. How are male and female roles presented in this Act?

_____

_____

_____

_____

_____

_____

_____

Question 4

> *"As she is mine, I may dispose of her:*
> *Which shall be either to this gentleman*
> *Or to her death, according to our law*
> *Immediately provided in that case."*

Explain the importance of this quote.

_____

_____

_____

_____

_____

_____

_____

_____

_____

*For questions 5-8, refer to **Act II Scene I.***

Question 5

Analyse the relationship between Oberon and Titania.

_____

_____

_____

_____

_____

_____

_____

_____

Question 6

How is the theme of jealousy explored?

_____

_____

_____

_____

_____

_____

_____

_____

_____

Question 7

Why do you think Shakespeare speaks about relationships in regards to the chaos happening around the world?

Question 8

> *"And thorough this distemperature we see*
> *The seasons alter: hoary-headed frosts*
> *Fall in the fresh lap of the crimson rose,*
> *And on old Hiem's thin and icy crown*
> *An odorous chaplet of sweet summer buds*
> *Is, as in mockery, set."*

How does Shakespeare's language create imagery? How does this fit in with the rest of Titania's speech?

----

*For questions 9-12, refer to **Act V Scene I.***

Question 9

The play ends with Robin's epilogue addressing the audience. How does an epilogue appeal to its audience? Why do you think Shakespeare ends *A Midsummer Night's Dream* in this way?

Question 10

Analyse the rhythm on the epilogue and how this is powerful for its audience.

Question 11

How is the theme of dreams explored in this final epilogue of *A Midsummer Night's Dream?*

_____

_____

_____

_____

_____

_____

_____

_____

_____

Question 12

In Act 5, Shakespeare uses several whimsical, light-hearted epilogues to end the play. However, in the previous Act, the audience witness conflict resolution, marriage and happiness.

Some could argue that Act V is unnecessary, because the narrative of *A Midsummer Night's Dream* has already been concluded.

Why do you think Shakespeare chooses to add this final Act to his play?

_____

_____

_____

_____

_____

_____

ESSAY QUESTIONS

1. What contrasts are conveyed in *A Midsummer Night's Dream?* Why are they important?

2. Why is the title, *A Midsummer Night's Dream*, important? How does this tie in with the overall narrative of the play?

3. Explore the nature of love conveyed in *A Midsummer Night's Dream*.

THE
REVISION
SERIES

INTRODUCTION TO POETRY

INTRODUCTION TO POETRY

SHAKESPEARE AND HIS POEMS

Aside from his literary genius in creating plays, William Shakespeare also spent a great deal of his writing career producing poems.

In total, Shakespeare wrote 154 sonnets, and five long narrative poems. His long narrative poems are less well-known, and he is mostly famous for his exceptional play writing skills and love poems.

LONG NARRATIVE POEMS

Shakespeare wrote five long narrative poems, each with a particular theme or subject topic in mind. These were written during different times throughout his writing career.

- *A Lover's Complaint*
- *Venus and Adonis*
- *The Rape of Lucrece*
- *The Phoenix and the Turtle*
- *The Passionate Pilgrim*

SONNETS

Shakespeare wrote 154 sonnets, each numbered (1-154).

Traditionally, a sonnet is a 14 line poem which is written in iambic pentameter. Shakespeare almost always used iambic pentameter when writing his sonnets.

What is Iambic Pentameter?

- Ten syllables to each line
- Five pairs of unstressed and stressed syllables (alternating)
      (Da dum, / da dum, / da dum, / da dum, / da dum)

Sometimes Shakespeare would break free from this, in order to add extra colour and feeling to his poetry.

INTRODUCTION TO POETRY

RHYMING PATTERNS

The rhyming pattern of English sonnets is as follows:

> a b a b ──────→ Lines 1 and 3 rhyme / lines 2 and 4 rhyme
>
> c d c d ──────→ Lines 5 and 7 rhyme / lines 6 and 8 rhyme
>
> efef ──────→ Lines 9 and 11 rhyme / lines 10 and 12 rhyme
>
> gg ──────→ Lines 13 and 14 rhyme

I have provided an example using Shakespeare's Sonnet 29, to emphasise the rhyming pattern:

SONNET 29

When in disgrace with Fortune and men's <u>eyes</u>,	**A**
I all alone beweep my outcast <u>state</u>,	**B**
And trouble deaf heaven with my bootless <u>cries</u>,	**A**
And look upon myself and curse my <u>fate</u>,	**B**
Wishing me like to one more rich in <u>hope</u>,	**C**
Featured like him, like him with friends <u>possessed</u>,	**D**
Desiring this man's art and that man's <u>scope</u>,	**C**
With what I most enjoy contented <u>least</u>,	**D**
Yet in these thoughts my self almost <u>despising</u>,	**E**
Haply I think on thee, and then my <u>state</u>,	**F**
(Like to the lark at break of day <u>arising</u>	**E**
From sullen earth) sings hymns at heaven's <u>gate</u>,	**F**
For thy sweet love remembered such wealth <u>brings</u>,	**G**
That then I scorn to change my state with <u>kings</u>.	**G**

Rhythm is a key technique used in poetry, in order to create emotions, mood and atmosphere.

Sonnets in particular use a beat to keep the momentum and flow of the narrative. For example, poems about love would have an upbeat, positive rhythm, whereas something more serious would have a very different beat.

INTRODUCTION TO POETRY

ANALYSING SONNETS

The first 126 sonnets in Shakespeare's collection appear to address a man. These sonnets deal with themes including love, nobility, music, time and betrayal.

Sonnets 127 to 152 appear to address a woman. The themes in language in these poem seem much more personal and intense compared to the first 126 sonnets.

The last two sonnets seem trivial. They appear to be written in a similar style to that of Greek epigrams. Although these poems do touch upon the relationship between Shakespeare and the woman (in sonnets 127 to 152), these two poems take a different turn in terms of language and narration.

When analysing sonnets, you should consider the following things:

- Narration
- Tone of voice
- 1st person or 3rd person
- Imagery
- Themes
- Rhythm
- Mood
- Feelings
- Structure
- Context

Shall I compare thee to a summer's day? Thou art more lovely and more temperate

William Shakespeare

POETRY TECHNIQUES IN HIS PLAYS

Shakespeare often used poetic devices in his plays. He did this on purpose and it proved really effective in theatre performances.

Most of Shakespeare's plays were written using iambic pentameter. He used this technique for the dialogue of higher-class characters. For lower-class characters, they would speak in prose as opposed to verses.

This would differentiate the social standings between different characters.

Poetry

PRACTICE QUESTIONS

*For questions 1-5, refer to **Sonnet 1.***

> "From fairest creatures we desire increase,
> That thereby beauty's rose might never die,
> But as the riper should by time decrease,
> His tender heir might bear his memory:
> But thou contracted to thine own bright eyes,
> Feed'st thy light's flame with self-substantial fuel,
> Making a famine where abundance lies,
> Thyself thy foe, to thy sweet self too cruel.
> Thou that art now the world's fresh ornament,
> And only herald to the gaudy spring,
> Within thine own bud buriest thy content,
> And, tender churl, mak'st waste in niggarding.
> Pity the world, or else this glutton be,
> To eat the world's due, by the grave and thee."

Question 1

Shakespeare explores this idea of beauty and nature. Find two quotes from the sonnet to demonstrate his ideas.

1. _____

2. _____

Question 2

What do the words *"rose"* and *"bud"* imply in this sonnet? What connotations are created?

_____

_____

_____

Question 3

Explain how Shakespeare explores the idea of time, using examples from the passage.

_____

_____

_____

_____

_____

_____

Question 4

What does line 2 in the sonnet mean? What theme is being conveyed?

_____

_____

_____

Question 5

"From fairest creatures we desire increase"

The use of the word *"increase"* could convey two possible meanings. The increase could be referring to commercial gain (i.e. money).

What other possible theme could the term "increase" suggest? Use another example from the sonnet to support your answer.

_____

_____

_____

---

*For questions 6-11, refer to **Sonnet 116**.*

"Let me not to the marriage of true minds
Admit impediments. Love is not love
Which alters when it alteration finds,
Or bends with the remover to remove:
O, no! it is an ever-fixed mark,
That looks on tempests and is never shaken.
It is the star to every wandering bark,
Whose worth's unknown, although his height be taken.
Love's not Time's fool, though rosy lips and cheeks
Within his bending sickle's compass come;
Love alters not with his brief hours and weeks,
But bears it out even to the edge of doom.
If this be error, and upon me proved,
I never writ, nor no man ever loved."

Question 6

Why do you think Shakespeare repeats words? For example *"love,"* *"alters"* and *"remove"*. What effect does this have on the reader?

_____

_____

_____

_____

Question 7

How does the poem explore the idea of love as a concept?

_____

_____

_____

_____

Question 8

Describe the structure of the sonnet. How does the final rhyming couplet shift the mood of the overall theme of the sonnet?

_____

_____

_____

_____

Question 9

How do you interpret the following line?

"Love is not love
Which alters when it alteration finds"

_____

_____

_____

_____

_____

Question 10

Shakespeare uses several metaphors in this sonnet to talk about nature. Find a metaphor and discuss the importance of this in relation to the themes implied in the sonnet.

_____

_____

_____

_____

Question 11

Find a quote to show Shakespeare's idea of the extreme.

_____

_____

For questions *12-15*, refer to **Sonnet 18.**

"Shall I compare thee to a summer's day?
Thou art more lovely and more temperate:
Rough winds do shake the darling buds of May,
And summer's lease hath all too short a date.
Sometime too hot the eye of heaven shines,
And often is his gold complexion dimm'd,
And every fair from fair sometime declines,
By chance, or nature's changing course, untrimm'd:
But thy eternal summer shall not fade,
Nor lose possession of that fair thou ow'st,
Nor shall death brag thou wander'st in his shade,
When in eternal lines to time thou grow'st,
So long as men can breathe, or eyes can see,
So long lives this, and this gives life to thee."

Question 12

How does this poem use language to express beauty?

Question 13

Why do you think the poem begins with a question?

Question 14

What does the phrase *"the eye of heaven"* imply?

_____

_____

_____

Question 15

Find a quote to show visual imagery and describe why Shakespeare has used this in his sonnet.

_____

_____

_____

_____

_____

_____

---
*For questions 16-20, refer to **Sonnet 7.***

"Lo, In the orient when the gracious light
Lifts up his burning head, each under eye
Doth homage to his new-appearing sight,
Serving with looks his sacred majesty;
And having climb'd the steep-up heavenly hill,
Resembling strong youth in his middle age,
Yet mortal looks adore his beauty still,
Attending on his golden pilgrimage:
But when from highmost pitch, with weary car,
Like feeble age, he reeleth from the day,
The eyes, 'fore duteous, now converted are
From his low tract, and look another way:
So thou, thyself outgoing in thy noon,
Unlooked on diest, unless thou get a son."

Question 16

The last word "son" is a play on the word "sun". Why does Shakespeare do this?

_____

_____

_____

Question 17

Give examples of religious imagery.

_____

_____

_____

Question 18

Why is the theme of procreation important in this sonnet?

_____

_____

_____

Question 19

How is the youth compared to the movement of the sun?

_____

_____

_____

Question 20

What does "Like feeble age, he reeleth from the day" mean?

_____

_____

_____

_____

_____

_____

ANSWERS -
ANALYSING PLAYS

OTHELLO

Q1.

The last two lines of Iago's speech reinforce his cunning and manipulative plan in order to bring down Othello. The fact that Iago states: *"But I will wear my heart upon my sleeve / For daws to peck at. I am not what I am,"* suggests that Iago is not what he seems. Shakespeare characterises Iago as a highly devious individual, who pretends to be something he is not, in order to achieve his goal (which is to destroy the relationship between Othello and Desdemona).

Q2.

Iago is implying that although he appears loving and obedient, he is only doing so in order to get what he wants. This not only allows the audience to establish who the villain is, but also reinforces the theme of appearance vs. reality. Iago is not who he appears to be – he is putting on an 'act'.

Q3.

This dialogue highlights Iago as being a manipulative, sly and cunning character. Jealousy is a prominent theme in *Othello* and is often the cause of Iago's behaviour. Iago appears to be someone he's not, in order to cause havoc and manipulate other characters, especially Othello. When Iago states, *"I follow him to serve my turn upon him,"* this clearly emphasises how Iago is taking advantage of Othello. His back-stabbing ways suggest to the audience/reader how Iago will go to any lengths in order to get what he wants.

Q4.

Shakespeare uses ironic language to emphasise how Iago's attempt at revenge is justifiable, because *"heaven is [his] judge."* This reference to heaven is ironic due to the fact that Iago's behaviour would not be acceptable in regards to religion. Heaven would not accept this behaviour, and therefore Iago tries to justify his actions by ironically saying how this is accepted in the name of God. The audience are able to see Iago's flaws before any action has occurred.

Q5.

When Othello claims that Desdemona's handkerchief is *"too little,"* not only could this be describing the size of the handkerchief, but it could also insinuate that Iago's cunning plan is beginning to work. Othello is beginning to have doubts about Desdemona's faithfulness, and therefore implying her handkerchief is too little suggests that their relationship is diminishing.

Q6.

Othello's soliloquy speaks about how Iago is *"honest"* and knowledgeable about *"human dealings."* Othello is unable to see Iago for what he is really is. He is oblivious to the fact that Iago wants him to doubt Desdemona. His soliloquy reinforces the consequences; if Iago's suspicions are proven correct. Othello is doubting Desdemona and discusses the importance of marriage and faithfulness.

Q7.

The phrase, *"I'd whistle her off,"* is used as a hunting term to suggest that Othello would wash his hands of his wife. It basically means 'I'll send her away' which reinforces how Iago has affected Othello's thoughts and opinions about Desdemona's loyalty.

Q8.

Iago's cunning plan is beginning to work, as Othello speaks about the ramifications if Desdemona has been unfaithful. Othello speaks about how he would *"whistle her off"* and *"loathe her."* Othello discusses marriage and how women *"belong to us,"* yet their desires and aspirations run wild. This implies that Iago is the reason why Othello is now presented as a conflicted character – Iago's attempt to control Othello is beginning to escalate and his plan is starting to work.

Q9.

Shakespeare uses the metaphor *"Nor scar that whiter skin of hers than snow."* Othello describes Desdemona's skin as being whiter than snow. The use of language allows imagery to be created, and the colour white reinforces the idea of purity, innocence, light and goodness.

Q10.

Othello's soliloquy is spoken quietly and he is no longer angry. Instead, he admires his sleeping wife and speaks about her beauty and smell. The sentence, *"Yet she must die"* implies that he feels obligated to kill her, as opposed to actually wanting to. The fact that *"He kisses her,"* reinforces his love for Desdemona. He states that he will love her after she is dead and restore the light/love.

Q11.

Othello's dialogue is used to contrast love and death. Shakespeare explores the idea of love through the use of language and refers to Desdemona as being a *"chaste star"*. However, Othello's language also draws upon ways of killing her and reinforces how he does not want to leave a scar or blood on her. These themes are integral to the narrative of *Othello*, and allow audiences to witness how love can be conflicting, challenging and unpredictable.

Q12.

Othello makes reference to light in his soliloquy. He enters with a candle and talks about *"Put[ting] out the light."* Othello could be implying two things here. The light going out could be used for dramatic effect on the audience watching. Alternatively, the light could be a symbol for Desdemona's life, and how Othello is planning on putting out the light (ending her life).

1. *One of the main themes Shakespeare highlights in Othello is the idea of doubt and betrayal. Using Othello's soliloquy from* **Act III Scene III** *and references from other Acts in the play, discuss the reasons why Othello suspects Desdemona of betrayal.*

- Othello begins to doubt Desdemona as a direct result of Iago's cunning plan to destroy their relationship.

- You should talk about how Iago constantly tries to manipulate Othello into believing his wife has been cheating on him.

- The fact that the play ends in the death of Othello and Desdemona signifies how Iago's plan has worked.

- In Othello's soliloquy, you can discuss how it is clear that he has doubts about Desdemona.

- You can talk about the handkerchief and how this is the beginning of Othello's concerns and Iago's cunning plan.

QUOTATIONS TO CONSIDER:

"If I do prove her haggard"
- Othello is beginning to question whether or not Desdemona has been faithful. He needs proof of her betrayal before he decides how to handle the situation.

"O curse of marriage"
- Othello is questioning their marriage.

"How shall I murder him, Iago?"
- Othello has been manipulated by Iago and wants to murder the man who he suspects of cheating with his wife.

"Your napkin is too little"
- This signifies how Othello has reservations about Desdemona. The fact that he is describing her handkerchief as too little suggests the decline in their relationship.

"But, O, what damned minutes tells her o'er
Who dotes, yet doubts, suspects, yet strongly loves!"
- Iago's reverse-psychology regarding Othello and the key theme of jealousy. Iago stirs up this idea that Othello should be jealous.

2. *Explain and analyse the importance of the role of women in the play, Othello. What effect does this have on audiences in the Elizabethan era compared to modern day?*

- In the play *Othello*, there are only three female roles – Desdemona, Emilia and Bianca.

- In Shakespearean times, women played a less than active role in society and were only perceived to be domesticated.

- Shakespeare highlights three pivotal characters in this play and how they play a significant role in the narrative of the play.

- The main female protagonist, Desdemona, is a pivotal character in regards to the main theme of jealousy and man's inability to trust. The fact that Desdemona remains consistent throughout the play in regards to her love for Othello is not enough to make her husband believe she is telling the truth.

- The play considers three different social standings of women. How do these roles differ from one another? What views do each of these characters have regarding love and marriage?

- You should talk about how women are perceived in Shakespearean times compared to that of today. Think about how values and traditions have changed in regards to gender roles. Have any of these gender roles stayed the same?

- The play conveys women as being one of two ways – pure and virtuous, or adulterous and sexually inclined. Why do you think Shakespeare conveys the women in this manner?

QUOTATIONS TO CONSIDER:

"Why, we have galls, and though we have some grace,
Yet have we some revenge. Let husbands know
Their wives have sense like them: they see, and smell,
And have their palates both for sweet and sour
As husbands have."

- Emilia speaking her real mind – standing up for women's rights.

"In Venice, they do not let God see the pranks / They dare not show their husbands. Their best conscience / Is not to leave't undone, but keep't unknown"

- Iago describing women of Venice. He suggests that women are deceptive and untrustworthy.

"She did deceive her father marrying you"
- Iago is implying that if Desdemona was able to deceive her father, there is no reason why she would not deceive her husband. This conveys women as being deceitful and disloyal.

3. *How is Iago represented throughout the play of Othello? Draw upon his relationship with other characters and how he is perceived by the audience.*

- Consider appearance vs. realism. Generally, what Iago says and what he means are two completely different things.
- His elaborate lies and cunning plans are at the centre of the play's action and the reason why Othello becomes jealous of his wife.
- Iago is consumed with jealousy, hatred and evil.
- He is conveyed as manipulative, sly, cunning and arrogant. He shows no true compassion to any of the characters, including his wife.
- The fact that characters often refer to him as being "honest Iago" highlights how Iago has got everyone to believe what he wants them to believe.
- He is represented as the character who is responsible for the fate of everyone else. The deaths of Desdemona and Othello are prime examples of Iago's behaviour throughtout the play.

QUOTATIONS TO CONSIDER:

"I am not what I am"
- This reinforces how Iago is not all what he appears. It's like he is two completely different people; the first being friendly and getting everyone to trust in him, but then turns into the villainous character who is deceitful, manipulative and cunning.

"Honest Iago"
- You can talk about how this description of Iago is ironic because in actual fact, he is far from honest during this play.

"We cannot all be masters, nor all masters / Cannot be truly follow'd"
- This foreshadows what's to come in the remaining narrative of the play. Iago is clearly stating how although he is following his master, not everything is as it seems, suggesting that he is going to back-stab Othello.

"What handkerchief!
Why, that the Moor first gave to Desdemona,
That which so often you did bid me steal"

- This shows how Iago has been planning revenge on Othello for a while. Iago attempts to steal the handkerchief as a way of using it against Desdemona, by showing how she has been unfaithful.

ROMEO AND JULIET

Q1.

The imagery conveyed in this passage is primarily religious. Both Romeo and Juliet use language which clearly makes reference to religion. This is established through the use of the words, *"holy shrine," "saints," "prayer"* and *"sin."* The use of religious imagery in Shakespeare's language conveys the idea of purity, and how the characters of Romeo and Juliet are drawn to one another, just as pilgrims are drawn to the holy shrine. At the time, religion played a huge role in society, and therefore audiences would be able to relate to this.

Q2.

The first 14 lines of this passage (up until Romeo kissing Juliet) read as a sonnet. Between the two, they confess their attraction towards one another. This reinforces the main theme of *Romeo and Juliet,* which is love. The whole narrative is centred around the concept of love, and the first meeting between the two lovers conveys this; through the use of poetic conventions. Just like a sonnet, these 14 lines read with passion in mind. The use of rhythm allows the audience to feel a sense of romance. The structure follows an AB rhyme scheme. For example, *"If I profane with my unworthiest hand / This holy shrine, the gentle sin is this: / My lips, two blushing pilgrims, ready stand / To smooth that rough touch with a tender kiss."* This shows how Shakespeare uses poetic techniques in order to emphasise themes such as love and passion.

Q3.

The phrase *"My unworthiest hand"* implies that Romeo does not deem himself as being a worthy suitor for Juliet. The fact that his hand is unworthy foreshadows conflict between his family (the Montagues) and her family (the Capulets).

Q4.

Shakespeare suggests that the sin which Romeo has committed by touching Juliet's hand needs to be erased, and so he wishes to make this up with a kiss. However, after their kiss, Juliet informs him that she is now in possession of his sin, and that he must kiss her again so she is free from the sin.

Q5.

The term "winged messenger" suggest angel-like features. Angels send messages down from heaven, and this is how Romeo sees Juliet, standing above him in the window.

Q6.

Personification

Q7.

Shakespeare compares day and night in this scene in order to demonstrate the good and bad in Romeo and Juliet's lives. It emphasises opposing forces in their relationship. This suggests that Romeo and Juliet's relationship could be seen as a struggle or conflict.

Q8.

"Two of the fairest stars in all the heaven / Having some business do entreat her eyes". This suggests that Romeo sees Juliet as being bright and as beautiful as the stars above. It shows Romeo's love for Juliet, by comparing her to something idyllic.

Q9.

The garden could symbolise freedom, peace and love. It could also represent innocence and purity.

Q10.

Romeo might be talking to Juliet from below her window, because he is not meant to be talking to her. He must remain hidden, which is why he is unable to simply knock on the door. This shows Romeo's dedication. Romeo has put himself in a vulnerable position, hence why he is positioned lower.

Q11.

After Juliet discovers Romeo's death, she takes it upon herself to sacrifice her life and die next to her *"true love."* Sacrifice is the perfect theme for a play based on romance and tragedy. This emphasises the sheer magnitude of the love Romeo and Juliet had for one another, and their longing to be with one another.

Q12.

The literal meaning of the poison is that it is the actual element that caused the death of Romeo. Symbolically, the poison acts as a visual aid for the destruction of Romeo and Juliet's relationship. The poison between their families as well as the poison (in literal terms), is a clear way of poisoning the love of Romeo and Juliet, which in the end results in their deaths.

1. *Using examples from Act II Scene II, and other examples from Romeo and Juliet, how does Shakespeare explore the relationship between Romeo and Juliet? Focus on language, imagery and themes.*

- You can talk about this idea of coming-of-age romance.

- You can discuss how they are both willing to defy their parents and run away with one another – despite the family feuds between her family and his.

- Their love is conveyed in a strong, poetic way.

- Find different quotes and examples that use specific themes and imagery in order to convey this idea of romance.

- Romeo continues to express his love throughout the play.

- The pivotal scenes, the balcony scene and the death scene, highlight the strength of their love. The death scene in particular shows how they are willing to do anything (including killing themselves) in order to be with one another.

- You can talk about how Shakespeare explores this idea of classic romantic love.

QUOTATIONS TO CONSIDER:
"You kiss by th' book"
- This shows how Juliet teases Romeo for being very conventional in his ways of 'wooing' her.

"It is too rash, too unadvis'd, too sudden"
- Juliet realises how quickly their romance has escalated. Not only does this show naivety and innocence, but it also shows the strength of their love for one another.

"Did my heart love till now? Forswear it, sight! For I ne'er saw true beauty till this night.
- Romeo questions whether he's been in love before (with Rosalind), after seeing Juliet for the very first time.

"My lips, two blushing pilgrims, ready stand
To smooth that rough touch with a tender kiss"

- The language used in the dialogue between Romeo and Juliet is romantic, expressive, and poetic. This use of language clearly captures the romance between these two characters, which is probably why the play *Romeo and Juliet* can be classed as one of the all-time best love stories in literary history.

2. *In what way does Romeo and Juliet break traditional gender conventions? Use examples from the play to support your answer.*

- In Shakespearean times, men would be classed as the dominant figure who would use violence, aggression and manipulation in order to defeat their opponents.

- Women were often objects for men to win after a conquest. They played a dismissive role, and would be subject to the male figure in their lives.

- The character of Romeo breaks free from traditional gender roles, by constantly being conveyed in a poetic manner.

- Romeo's masculinity is challenged throughout the play due to his feminine traits and language used. This is particularly true when it comes to his relationship with Juliet.

- Juliet is often conveyed as an independent, strong-minded woman.

- Although Romeo does defend his family, and does show signs of masculinity in terms of violence and aggression (the killing of Tybalt), as the male protagonist, he is still conveyed in a way that is not as masculine as other male protagonists in Shakespeare's works.

QUOTATIONS TO CONSIDER:

"Love is a smoke made with the fumes of sighs, / Being purg'd , a fire sparkling in lovers' eyes"

- This reinforces the poetic dialogue Romeo would use to express his feelings for Juliet. In terms of masculinity, this breaks free from traditional gender roles, as men would be viewed as figures who are strong and dominant – but the fact that Romeo expresses his views, shows his weakness (his love for Juliet) and therefore detracts from his masculinity.

"O, speak again, bright angel, for thou art / As glorious to this night, being o'er my head"

- This is a physical representation of women being more in control than men. The fact that Romeo is positioned lower than Juliet (Juliet is above in the window, whereas Romeo is standing on the ground outside), illustrates the change in gender roles.

"If that thy bent of love be honourable, / Thy purpose marriage, send me word to-morrow"

- Juliet breaks free from traditional female stereotypes. The fact that she is unmarried and quite forward in her dialogue reinforces her independence and strong-mindedness. At the time in which the play was written, this type of behaviour from women was deemed unacceptable and abnormal.

3. *Discuss how Juliet's maturity levels change from the beginning of the play to the end of the play. Why does her maturity change? What impact does this have on the audience? Why is this important to the narrative?*

- You should discuss how Juliet's character changes as the play progresses.

- At the beginning of the play, we view Juliet's character to be young, naïve, innocent and pure.

- As her love continues to blossom for Romeo, we see how Juliet's character becomes more developed.

- You need to explain why you think Shakespeare shows Juliet's maturity levels changing. Do you think it allows you to see transformations of age? Do you think Shakespeare wants you to relate to the changes that every person goes through from childhood to adolescence? Is there any other reasons why you think Shakespeare does this?

- Explain the impact this has on the audience. Showing the changes in maturity levels not only links back to the theme of coming-of-age, but also creates quite a fast-paced rhythm for the overall narrative.

QUOTATIONS TO CONSIDER:

"It is an honour that I dream not of"

- When Juliet's mother asks her about her views on marriage (at the beginning of the play), Juliet's response highlights how she has not begun to think about love or marriage as of yet.

"If he be married, / My grave is likely to be my wedding bed"

- After seeing Romeo at the ball, Juliet's views towards love and marriage begin to change. As the audience/reader, we see how her maturity levels are beginning to change, and how she is changing from a young girl into a young woman.

"Shall I speak ill of him that is my husband?

As, poor my lord, what tongue shall smooth thy name

When I, thy three-hours' wife, have mangled it?"

- Here, we see Juliet recognising that love is not all plain-sailing. Instead, she starts to show understanding that difficulties and challenges lie ahead in marriage.

MACBETH

Q1.

The sentence *"False face must hide what the false heart doth know"* presents the idea of appearance vs. reality. Macbeth is talking about how you have to hide your falseness by putting on a pretend face.

Q2.

Gender roles seem to be quite controversial when contrasting the characters of Macbeth and his wife. In Lady Macbeth's speech, she is clearly taking the dominant role. She is the one who is conveyed as strong-minded, opinionated and confident. This contrasts with Macbeth's character, who seems to be portrayed as quite passive and uncertain. Therefore, this clearly shows a change in role reversals whereby the male characters are usually portrayed as the superior, and the women are portrayed as inferior.

Q3.

The sentence, *"Bring forth men-children only, / For thy undaunted mettle should compose / Nothing but males,"* reinforces the idea of a misogynistic culture. Lady Macbeth has been conveyed as a dominant, masculine, power-driven woman. Shakespeare explores the idea of misogyny during the sixteenth century, but challenges the idea of male and female roles. Lady Macbeth possesses her own masculine authority, which would be fit for raising male children. This is something audiences would be interested in, as hierarchy and gender roles were significant at the time this play was written.

Q4.

"I am settled" reinforces how Macbeth has been persuaded by his wife to undergo their plan of murder. His persuasive, dominant wife has taken control over the situation and manipulated her husband with thoughts of power, greed and control.

Q5.

Lady Macbeth makes continued reference to blood during this Act. The fact that she is trying to *"wash her hands"* of that *"damned spot"* suggests the idea of bloody hands. This is not literal, and instead, is used metaphorically as a way of conveying her guilty conscience. When someone is said to have bloody hands, they usually have something to admit, and have done wrong. The fact that she knows her *"hands ne'er be clean"* reinforces how she has to live with what she has done.

Q6.

Lady Macbeth's sleepwalking shows her physical decline in strength and power. Sleepwalking is a condition that you are unable to control. It puts you in a vulnerable position both emotionally and physically. This emphasises that Lady Macbeth is no longer in control of her thoughts and behaviour.

Q7.

The themes that are conveyed in this extract include the decline of power and guilt. Lady Macbeth is depicted as a vulnerable character who is unable to deal with the guilt she feels, from the murders she's committed. This highlights her downward spiral, and how everything she has done was not worth it.

Q8.

The main sense that can be conveyed in this extract is sight, or a lack of sight if you will. The fact that Lady Macbeth is sleepwalking suggests that her sight has been jeopardised. This suggests to the audience that the character of Lady Macbeth is slowly declining, and is no longer the powerful, dominant character she once was.

Q9.

Shakespeare shows the audience the defeat of Macbeth using the stage direction *"Enter Macduff with Macbeth's head."* This allows the audience to have a clear visual of evil being defeated. Not only does this create a dramatic impact for the audience, but this also reinforces the play of *Macbeth* as being a tragedy.

Q10.

The word *"tyrant"* is used to describe the character of Macbeth as being a cruel and oppressive ruler. This reinforces how the audience see Macbeth as the protagonist, as well as the villain of the play. Other characters in *Macbeth* show how they feel about the character of Macbeth by implying that he was not considered a beloved ruler. This is also emphasised by all of the characters stating *"Hail, King of Scotland"* for Malcolm – showing little compassion for the death of Macbeth.

Q11.

Kingship vs. tyranny is paramount in the final Act, and this is best shown by comparing the characters of Macbeth and Macduff. Macbeth was power-driven and considered a *"tyrant"*. Other characters (and the audience) see him as being oppressive, greedy and oppressive. In contrast, Macduff is noble, and attempts to rectify the damage caused by Macbeth. He is hoping to create harmony and honour, and wishes to be respected. This clearly indicates the difference between honourable Kingship and cruel tyranny.

Q12.

The play clearly emphasises the importance of evil and defeat. Macbeth and Lady Macbeth are clear examples of how evil is defeated. Although they are the main characters in the play, they are inflicted with power, control, manipulation and evil. They commit a series of murders in order to move one step closer to a stronger position within society. However, we slowly see these characters spiralling downwards. As the narrative progresses, we see Lady Macbeth losing her mind and sleepwalking. This reinforces her guilty conscience and inability to continue with her life the way it is. Macbeth is defeated and killed, which shows resolution. Both characters are prime examples of evil, villainous characters who are defeated for the greater good.

1. *How much is Macbeth the victim of his own fate? How does his character spiral downwards as the play progresses?*

- This answer will be based on how much you believe Macbeth is the victim of his own fate.

- For example, you could argue that Macbeth is purely to blame for how his fate pans out in the play.

- The fact that Macbeth thrives on power and control is the reason why his character down spirals. He is unable to control the power that he has been given, and is unable to rule without evil and ego getting in the way.

- He is led and influenced by his wife's ambitions to rule Scotland. He is heavily influenced by Lady Macbeth, and he chooses to accept what she tells him to do.

- You could argue whether you think fate was to blame or whether you think someone else was to blame (was it the witches' fault for telling Macbeth about the prophecies?)

- The audience/reader see a visual decline in Macbeth's character after the murders he commits to withhold power. Things to talk about include the dagger, hallucinations and blood. This foreshadows Macbeth's own death.

QUOTATIONS TO CONSIDER:
"Is this a dagger which I see before me?
The handle toward my hand? Come, let me clutch thee.
I have thee not, and yet I see thee still"
- This quote is a visual declination of Macbeth's character. The dagger that Macbeth is hallucinating foreshadows the bloody path to his own death.

"Sleep no more! Macbeth does murder sleep"
- This shows Macbeth's mental declination. The fact that Macbeth is hearing voices signifies how the choices he has made has led to his downfall.

2. *Discuss the influence of the witches' prophecies and how this stirs the action that occurs in the play.*

- The witches' prophecies are clear ammunition which instigate Macbeth's ambition to become King of Scotland.

- The fact that the witches' first prophecy that he will become Thane of Cawdor becomes reality, gives reason for Macbeth to believe their other prophecies will also come true.

- Consider the metaphor of the storm at the beginning of the play (in relation to the sailor) and how this foreshadows the unpredictable events that will occur in Macbeth's life.

- The witches' curse on the sailor replicates the same fate for Macbeth.

QUOTATIONS TO CONSIDER:

"All hail, Macbeth, that shalt be king hereafter!"
- This is the first incident where Macbeth is told about his future to be king.

"What? Can the Devil speak true?"
- After the first prophecy comes true, Banquo and Macbeth are confused and intrigued about the witches' prophecies. The fact that the first prophecy has come true signifies how Macbeth's fate has been chosen for him.

"This supernatural soliciting / Cannot be ill; cannot be good"
- Macbeth is weary, sceptical and weighing up these events. This is the beginning of how Macbeth's life is going to pan out – it foreshadows how he will continue to be sceptical and weighing up his options in order to maintain power.

3. *Explore the theme of the supernatural. Pay attention to key ideas including hallucinations and ghosts, the role of the witches and the floating dagger. Why is the theme of the supernatural important to the tragic story of Macbeth?*

- The play *Macbeth* shows three witches who are able to predict the future and control the weather. This provides a sense of magic and supernatural – creating an intriguing and mystic atmosphere.

- At the time of writing, supernatural was a fascinating topic for the majority of people. Many of the people believed in some form of witchcraft or supernatural element.

- Hallucinations play a crucial role in the play. Both the characters of Macbeth and Lady Macbeth suffer from extreme hallucinations.

- The floating dagger not only illustrates the violence of the play, but also acts as a symbol of Macbeth's guilty conscience. It is a reminder of Macbeth's actions and how this triggers the dramatic events of the narrative.

QUOTATIONS TO CONSIDER:

"I have thee not, and yet I see thee still art thou not, fatal vision, sensible to feeling as to sight? Or art though but a dagger of the mind, a false creation, proceeding from the heat-oppressed brain?"

- This quote shows Macbeth talking to the floating dagger. Macbeth is questioning whether he should kill the king. The supernatural element is based on the fact that he can see the dagger but can't touch it – is he able to kill the King of Scotland?

"Thy bones are marrowless, thy blood is cold; Thou hast no speculation in those eyes, which thou dost glare with"

- Here, Macbeth is spooked by the ghost of Banquo. The use of the supernatural allows Macbeth's character to visually decline in front of the audience's eyes and emphasise revenge. Macbeth told the dining guests that Banquo was simply running late, however Macbeth knows full well what he has done, and the ghost is a visual reminder of his bloody hands.

"Into the air, and what seem'd corporal melted as breath into the wind. Would they had stay'd?"

- This quote signifies the witches' prophecies and how the witches travel by vanishing into thin air. Along with the three prophecies that the witches have predicted, this shows how supernatural plays a huge role in the events of the play.

AS YOU LIKE IT

Q1.

Alliteration 1 = *"painted pomp"*

Alliteration 2 = *"And churlish chiding of the winter's wind"*

Effect = the use of alliteration allows rhythm and mood to be created.

Q2.

Duke Senior explores the idea of pastoral imagery through the use of his language. He uses words such as *"seasons,"* and *"winter's winds"* to emphasise nature and atmosphere. He compares the *"painted pomp"* of the courts with the forest. The forest is written in a romanticised way, expressing the *"good in everything".* Pastoral imagery is used to create a sense of mood and atmosphere which helps to set the scene in which the narrative is set. This allows the audience to have a clear visualisation of the surroundings.

Q3.

The Duke is saying how the forests make him feel like himself. The fact that he says *"These are counsellors that feelingly persuade me what I am"*, reinforces how the forests are like a counsellor, which allow you to open up and be yourself. This is ironic, because the forests contain people who pretend to be someone else.

Q4.

The Duke is comparing life of the civilised world with the forest. In the forest, the Duke describes the beauty of the forest through the use of language. He highlights sounds and images that are created through nature, which allows imagery and mood to be created.

Q5.

The sentence *"I rather will subject me to the malice of a diverted blood and bloody brother,"* suggests that the relationship between Orlando and Oliver is quite hostile. The fact that Oliver is trying to get rid of Orlando by killing him is reinforced through the use of the word *"blood."* Orlando states that he would rather give himself up to his violent brother, as opposed to running away.

Q6.

Shakespeare's language *"when service sweat for duty, not for mead"* reinforces how people used to work because it was their duty, as opposed to simply working for money. This is completely different to modern day society. In modern times, people work to provide for themselves and their families, whereas years ago people worked for pleasure and obligation.

Q7.

The relationship between Orlando and Adam is really amicable. Adam is older than Orlando and has good intentions to try and protect Orlando from his brother. He offers his savings for Orlando to start over somewhere new. The fact that Adam states *"let me be your servant. Though I look old, yet I am strong and lusty"* reinforces how Adam attempts to provide help to his friend. He also states that he will work for his *"master"*. This shows a close relationship. We can see that it's not just based on a servant and master working relationship, but that they are also friends.

Q8.

In Adam's speech, beginning with *"Master, go on, and I will follow thee,"* Shakespeare uses rhyming couplets. Shakespeare uses these rhyming couplets as a way of emphasising the noble and decent characteristics of Adam. Although he is a servant, the fact that Shakespeare has chosen to use a rhyming pattern for this character suggests that he is deemed important and righteous. This creates a powerful image for the audience, by providing lower class citizens with characteristics that are often conveyed in higher class people.

Q9.

Shakespeare ends the play *As You Like It* using an epilogue from Rosalind, in order to go against convention. Generally, a male character would give the epilogue at the end of the play. However, Shakespeare uses a woman in this instance to emphasise how gender roles are often unionised. The fact that the play is full of gender transformations, shows how Shakespeare plays with gender roles and appearance.

Q10.

"It is not the fashion to see the lady the epilogue, but it is no more unhandsome than to see the lord the prologue". This emphasises how Shakespeare explores gender roles and appearance, by conveying characters as being a different gender. Rosalind is saying how it's no worse seeing a women give the epilogue, compared to a man giving the prologue. Shakespeare is trying to subvert conventions and go against tradition.

Q11.

Rosalind claims that she is *"not furnished like a beggar; therefore to beg will become me."* This basically describes the importance of appearance and how this affects behaviour and speech. Rosalind is addressing the audience by saying how, because she is not dressed like a beggar, she is not going to beg for acceptance.

Q12.

Although the character of Rosalind changes from man to woman throughout the play, it is likely that her character is actually played by a man. In Shakespearean times, it was common for men to play female roles in theatre. The fact that Rosalind stats *"if I were a woman"* implies that she isn't actually a woman.

1. *Discuss the theme of family in As You Like It. Support your answer using two or more characters as an example.*

- Two key characters you can talk about in relation to family are Orlando and his brother Oliver.

- At the beginning of the play, we see how Orlando is ready for a mutiny with his brother. This highlights other key themes including conflict, revenge and disloyalty.

- In Act 1 Scene 1, we also are shown an argument between the two brothers. Orlando argues with Oliver about how he has been treated since the death of their father.

- You can talk about the power struggle in their family relationship. Both are male characters, and therefore try to exert some kind of power and control over the situations that arise.

- Despite the conflict and constant arguments, the family bond is ignited when Orlando saves Oliver's life from a lion. This reinforces how Orlando possesses characteristics of selflessness and bravery, and overall shows brotherly love.

- Orlando's behaviour causes Oliver to transform himself into a better person, and a better brother. Oliver feels ashamed at how he has treated his brother since the death of their father.

- Family treachery – Orlando (the younger brother) and Oliver (the eldest brother). Oliver inherited everything after the death of their father, and treated his younger brother unfairly.

QUOTATIONS TO CONSIDER:

"Marry, sir, I am helping you to mar that which God / made, a poor unworthy brother of yours, with idleness

- Orlando is talking to his brother about how their relationship is tainted. It also draws on religious imagery to mark how their behaviour has been unacceptable.

Stage direction – *Strikes him*

- Oliver lashes out at his brother which emphasises the conflict between the two brothers.

"I never loved my brother in my life"

- Oliver claims how he has never loved his brother. This clearly demonstrates the tension and conflict between the two brothers.

2. *How is Orlando's and Rosalind's relationship portrayed? Consider the use of language and imagery.*

- The relationship between Rosalind and Orlando is central to the topic of love.

- Rosalind falls in love after she watches Orlando wrestle with Charles. This shows how Rosalind falls in love with someone she hasn't got to know.

- The fact that Rosalind is disguised for the majority of the play as a man, whilst in pursuit of Orlando, suggests how their relationship began in an untraditional sense.

- Their love is articulated through the use of poetic language. This is emphasised by the carvings left for one another on trees in the forest.

- Rosalind and Orlando only meet a couple of times without the disguise of Ganymede. How then, could they possibly be in true love? You can discuss how the disguise of Rosalind makes their love questionable.

QUOTATIONS TO CONSIDER:

"The truest poetry is the most feigning"

- Touchstone describes the love of Rosalind and Orlando as being dishonest and misguided. Did they rush into their relationship? Were these two characters blindsided by one another? Is their love real or are they more fascinated with the idea of love rather than being in love?

"Men have died from time to time, and worms have eaten them, but not for love"

- Rosalind rejects Orlando's statement that he will die if she didn't love him in return. This shows the sheer magnitude of Orlando's feelings for Rosalind.

"O Rosalind! These trees shall be my books / And in their barks my thoughts I'll character"

- This is a visual depiction of how Orlando expresses his love for Rosalind by marking his words into the trees bark.

"Sir you have wrestled well, and overthrown / More than your enemies"

- Rosalind falls in love with Orlando at first sight. This is also shown by her giving him her necklace.

"My affection hath an unknown bottom"

- Again, this shows the strength of the love that Rosalind carries for Orlando.

3. *How does Shakespeare use language to emphasise class differences between the characters? Why is this important to Shakespearean audiences?*

- Class hierarchy:
  - Upper class = Rosalind, Oliver, Orlando, Celia, Dukes
  - Peasants = Silvius, Audrey, Corin, Phoebe
- Orlando is unable to be with Rosalind at the beginning of the play because of his misfortune (Oliver, his elder brother, inherited everything after the death of their father.)
- Orlando was able to marry Rosalind with the fortune Oliver gives to him after their reconciliation.
- The social classes conveyed seem to change as the play progresses.
- The stereotype of the fool is highly disregarded by the courts, but plays a huge role in the play by providing comical value for the audience and other characters.

QUOTATIONS TO CONSIDER:

"Your accent is something finer than you could purchase in so removed a dwelling"

- This reinforces the idea of class differences. The way characters talk is a huge influence on how the characters social standing is perceived.

"He keeps me rustically at home or, to speak more properly, stays me here at home unkept; for call you that keeping for a gentleman of my birth that differs not from the stalling of an ox?"

- This shows how Orlando and Oliver are represented in different ways. The fact that Oliver has kept Orlando from receiving education, has affected how Orlando is perceived in terms of social standing. He is considered less than a gentlemen due to the fact that he is uneducated and not wealthy.

- Although Orlando and Oliver come from the same family background, the fact that Oliver has received the fortune of their dead father, shows how the two characters are presented in opposing social standings. Oliver is represented as being highly fortunate, whereas Orlando has no means in terms of commodity or education.

THE TAMING OF THE SHREW

Q1.

Petruchio repeats Kate's name several times. The fact that he repeats her name is emphasising how he is in control of her. He uses her name as a way of showing Katherina that he holds power and dominance. Addressing her directly shows his affection, although this could be seen as undermining and child-like.

Q2.

Petruchio's attempt to woo Katherina suggests that he is trying to counteract everything she says in order to assert his authority. For example, Petruchio claims the following: *"Say that she frown, I'll say she looks as clear as morning roses newly wash'd with dew. Say she be mute and will not speak a word, then I'll commend her volubility and say she uttereth piercing eloquence".* This reinforces how he will antagonise her, hoping that she falls for his determination and willingness to stick by her.

Q3.

Petruchio repeats her name by addressing her as "Kate", even after she states that everyone should address her as Katherina. Again, this shows his attempts to antagonise her, and his affection for her.

Q4.

There is a clear power struggle in the relationship between Katherina and Petruchio. Katherina is shown to be an independent woman, who says what she thinks. She refuses to be dominated by male figures. The fact the Petruchio attempts to dominate her, shows that he is in control of her. In modern society, the saying that 'opposites attract' could be applied to their relationship; the fact that they are completely opposite to one another suggests that they are a perfect match.

Q5.

Petruchio's ridiculous attire to his wedding symbolises the control he maintains over his future wife, Katherina. This humiliates Katherina. The fact that Katherina has no choice but to marry him makes it even more shameful and embarrassing for both her and her family. This reinforces Petruchio's authority, and how he is the dominant figure in their relationship.

Q6.

The line *"not so well apparell'd as I wish you were"* suggests that Petruchio is not very well dressed. The fact that he has shown up to his wedding in old clothes, reinforces this. Tranio's response reinforces common beliefs regarding certain attire when appearing at a wedding, especially if you are the groom.

Q7.

You could have any response, and you could agree or disagree with the statement that Baptista would go to any lengths to get his daughter married.

For example:

You could argue that the fact Baptista overlooks Petruchio's silly and informal clothing suggests that he is just glad that someone wants to marry his "shrew" of a daughter.

Q8.

Petruchio's language shows that he is eager to see his future wife. He askes *"where is Kate? Where is my love?"* Not only does this show his affection towards Katherina, but it could also suggest that he is ready to begin a marriage based on male dominance and antagonistic behaviour. The sentence *"some comet or unusual prodigy"* implies that the other characters (especially Baptista) are looking at him weirdly (due to his choice in clothing). Therefore, Petruchio's clothing is being viewed as people view a comet – surprised and questionable.

Q9.

Simile 1 = *"A woman mov'd is like a fountain troubled"*

Explanation = Katherina compares the role of a woman as being like a troubled fountain. Although fountains look beautiful and graceful, they can be agitated and unpleasant – much like a woman.

Simile 2 = *"Confounds thy fame as whirlwinds shake fair buds"*

Explanation = 'confounds thy fame' basically suggests destruction of reputation. This destruction is compared to a whirlwind which is unpredictable. However the words "fair buds" implies innocence and gives this idea of femininity being destroyed by a stronger force (whirlwind = men).

Q10.

This sentence reinforces how women are not perceived as strong as men. Women are presented as being *"soft"* and *"weak"* and therefore are troubled in the world. This reinforces how male figures are supposed to be the more dominant figure in society, which is why Katherina needs to be "tamed" by a man.

Q11.

*You could have any response, and you could agree or disagree with the statement that Katherina has transformed completely from the final Act compared to the rest of the play.

<u>For example:</u>

You could argue how Katherina is now tamed, due to her new duties/responsibilities towards her husband. In Katherina's final epilogue, she claims that she now has *"such duty as the subject owes the prince, even such a woman oweth to her husband"*. This reinforces how she uses royalty imagery to address her husband. The fact that she will stand and place *"[her] hands below [her] husband's foot"* reinforces the superiority men have over women. Katherina is no longer presented as the independent and aggressive "shrew". She is now a character physically and emotionally undermined by the man.

Q12.

Even in the title, the word "taming" highlights how a person is to be domesticated. Petruchio continues to cure Katherina's aggressive behaviour by domesticating her into the well-rounded, dutiful wife. Katherina is shown to slowly become domesticated by obeying her husband and showing how she is "in token of which duty, if he please, [her] hand is ready, may it do him ease." This reinforces how Katherina has been controlled and manipulated into a woman who obeys her husband, and follows the traditional stereotypes of the time at which the play was set.

1. *Compare and contrast the theme of reality vs. appearance in The Taming of the Shrew.*

- There are many occurrences of whereby reality versus appearance is apparent in *The Taming of the Shrew.*

- Within this play, we see physical disguises of certain characters, deceptive and psychological changes in behaviour, and changes in attitude and actions.

- For example:

  o Lucentio disguised as a tutor, in hope to woo Bianca.

  o Tranio disguised as his master (Lucentio).

  o Hortensio disguised as a tutor, in hope to woo Bianca.

  o Katherina's transition from a shrew to a tamed wife.

  o Bianca's ability to appear sweet and innocent, but also has characteristics similar to her sister.

- Another example of appearance that plays a crucial element in the relationship between Katherina and Petruchio, is Petruchio's wedding costume. His old-fashioned clothing was worn to embarrass Katherina and make the point that he is in control.

- Bianca appears to be a goody-two-shoes who is only interested in her education. Yet, her private tutoring lessons see Bianca flirt with male suitors.

QUOTATIONS TO CONSIDER:

"And place your hands below your husband's foot"

- This reinforces how Katherina is conveyed as being tamed at the end of the play. Is this accurate? Or do you think Katherina is putting on an appearance?

Stage direction – *Enter Tranio disguised as Lucentio and the Merchant, booted and bare headed, dressed like Vincentio.*

- This shows how characters are appearing to be people that they are not. This is a visual depiction of the theme reality vs. appearance.

"And yet I come not well"

- This quote signifies how Petruchio has come dressed poorly to his wedding to Katherina. This emphasises how his appearance suggests how he wants to humiliate Katherina. The reality is, Katherina has to marry him because nobody else wants to marry a 'shrew'.

"Fie, what a foolish duty call you this?"

- Bianca also carries characteristics as being a shrew, just like her sister. She tries to resist being controlled by a male figure (Lucentio).

2. *Explore the main criticism that Shakespeare represents women as being "objects". To what extent of this is true? Why do you think Shakespeare chooses to represent his female characters in this way?*

- This question will be based on our personal understanding of *The Taming of the Shrew*.

- You will need to mention how women in society, based on when this play was written, were stereotyped as being domesticated and in need of a husband. In the Elizabethan era, women had little rights, and were subject to their father or husband.

- This play examines the 16th century ideas about gender and equality issues.

- You can discuss how women are placed in a role whereby they are assumed to act a certain way towards men and marriage.

- For example, you can say how Katherina is placed under the power and control of her husband Petruchio. The way Katherina is portrayed in relation to marriage, is significantly different to how she was conveyed when she was an independent, single woman. You can say how her behaviour in the beginning of the play would be frowned upon, as it doesn't adhere to the traditional gender roles of women.

- Katherina is an "object" both to her father and to her husband. Her father uses her as a way of maintaining their family status. The fact that her father needs her to marry signifies the importance of marriage. Women were deemed to be more respected if they had a husband and followed traditional patriarchal values.

- The character of Bianca is also conveyed as an "object", but much to her amusement. She flirts with her male suitors and soon becomes the "object" in her relationship with Lucentio.

- Bianca is also the object to her father's ambition to trade her off for profit.

- These examples are all visual aids of how women are controlled and manipulated by the male power, and therefore shown as being less than equal.

QUOTATIONS TO CONSIDER:

"To seek their fortunes father than at home"

- Petruchio suggests this idea that he is not only looking for a wife, but commodity too.

"Will undertake to woo curst Katherine, / Yea and to marry her, if her dowry please"

- This reinforces the control that Petruchio is soon to have over Katherina.

"Thy husband is thy lord, thy life, thy keeper"

- This rule of three suggests how Katherina has now been tamed and manipulated by the male power.

"Come sit on me"

- A sexual innuendo used to frustrate Katherina, and show how Petruchio is in control of the situation.

3. *Compare and contrast the two sisters, Katherina and Bianca, using examples from both the beginning of the play and the end of the play. What do you learn from each character and why is this important to the overall narrative of The Taming of the Shrew?*

- There are two parts to be answered to score highly for this question. Firstly, you need to compare the characters of Katherina and Bianca. Secondly, you need to analyse the importance of their role within the overall narrative of *The Taming of the Shrew*.

- Let's begin by looking at how Katherina is portrayed:

   o In the opening Acts, Katherina is described as being "curst". She is conveyed as being bad-tempered, independent and challenges this idea of patriarchal values.

   o She speaks her mind and degrades men.

- o She is met by a man who challenges her behaviour and values. Some might say that he is of an equal match for her – both intelligent, feisty, domineering etc.

- o As the play progresses, the audience/reader see Katherina's character change from being unpleasant and ill-tempered, to a wife who shows respect and submissiveness towards her husband.

- Now let's look at the character of Bianca:

- o Bianca is the younger of the two sisters, and is made out to be sweet and naïve.

- o Due to the fact that she appears to be well-spoken, respectful and endearing, is stereotypical to how women were perceived in Elizabethan times. This is the reason why Bianca has many male suitors, because her behaviour and personality is what is expected from a future wife.

- o However, some of her characteristics, like flirting with her suitors and teasing Kate, suggests that she is not all that she appears.

- Their relationship shows how Katherina has control of her sister (by tying her hands up) and showing the dominant and submissive.

QUOTATIONS TO CONSIDER:

"I prithee, sister Kate, untie my hands"
- This shows the position of submission. The two sisters are represented in completely opposing ways.

Stage direction – *She strikes her*
- Again, this shows Katherina's control over her sister. It also shows Katherina's aggressive and ill-tempered nature.

"She is your treasure, she must have a husband. / I must dance barefoot on her wedding day"
- This could imply how Katherina feels left out. Her father favours Bianca more than her. To dance barefoot is traditional behaviour for an unmarried woman whose younger sister is getting married before her. This implies how Katherina sees no future in finding someone who wants to marry her.

A MIDSUMMER NIGHT'S DREAM

Q1.

This extract uses the image of moonlight, to great effect. The moon is a way for Theseus to monitor the time until he is married to Hippolyta. In Theseus's dialogue, he claims that the moon is moving too slowly and that this is preventing his marriage to Hippolyta. In contrast, Hippolyta's dialogue emphasises how the moon is moving quickly into the new phase. This is relevant to the play because not only is the moonlight a way of emphasising the 'night', but it also highlights the idea of transitioning from one phase to another.

Q2.

"Stand forth, Demetrius. – My noble lord, / This man hath my consent to marry her. – / Stand forth, Lysander. – And my gracious duke, /This man hath bewitched the bosom of my child." This reinforces the idea of arranged marriage, which suggests that this was common at the time at which the play was written and performed. Shakespeare draws upon traditions and values in order to appeal to his targeted audiences, many of whom would relate to the idea of being forced to marry someone. Marriage is therefore conveyed as a chore, as opposed to being about love.

Q3.

Feminine roles are significantly different to those of masculine roles. Women in this play are bound by marriage, which is often chosen for them by their fathers. In this extract, Egeus is talking to Theseus about his longing for his daughter to marry Demetrius. Instead, his daughter Hermia has fallen in love with someone else, Lysander. The fact that if she rejects his choice, her father would rather her die, suggests the level of power men had over women's choices and independence.

Q4.

This quote reinforces the ramifications of disobeying a male figure, at the time at which the play was set. If Hermia chooses to disobey her father, he can lawfully have her killed. There is a clear contrast here between traditions in this era, compared to modern-day society. The fact that the male figure chooses the husband for his daughter or has her killed, reinforces the dominance and power that men had in society.

Q5.

The relationship between Oberon and Titania is far from loving. Although they are King and Queen of the fairyland, the language between them is extremely hostile. The fact that they enter from either side of the stage as opposed to entering together, reinforces the characters separation (physically and emotionally).

Q6.

The theme of jealousy is apparent through this extract, especially since Titania and Oberon are accusing one another of being unfaithful. Titania comes out directly and accuses Oberon of being *"jealous"* and talks about his *"buskined mistress"*. Oberon states how she cannot accuse him when she is in *"love to Theseus"*.

Q7.

Shakespeare compares relationships with the chaos going on around the world, to demonstrate that love and marriage are never plain-sailing. Titania also addresses this chaos as being a direct result of their arguments. She states how *"this same progeny of evil comes / From our debate, from our dissension. / We are their parents and originals."* The realm of the fairies, and the arguments between Titania and Oberon, are having an effect on the *"human mortals."*

Q8.

Shakespeare uses language in this extract in order to convey seasonal imagery. The use of the words *"frosts"* and *"sweet summer buds"* creates visual imagery for the audience. It shows the transitions between the seasons and how different moods and feelings can be generated from each season.

Q9.

An epilogue allows a character to speak directly to the audience. The character can sum up the overall message of the play and generate a response from the audience. In this play, the epilogue uses dreams. This is the perfect ending; it fits in with the title of the play.

Q10.

The rhythm of the epilogue uses rhyming couplets as its final dialogue in the play. This creates an upbeat rhythm for the audience and provides a sense of light-hearted, fun interaction between character and audience. Using a tight rhyme scheme, it reinforces the idea that Shakespeare is tying up loose ends using memorable dialogue. Shakespeare addresses the audience using direct dialogue, by establishing the fact that it is a comedy, whereas other plays of Shakespeare (such as tragedies) end in a very different way with no happy or theatrical ending.

Q11.

The theme of dreams is explored in the epilogue, as Puck addresses how the audience should perceive the play as a dream – if they were not contented. The fact that he states: *"While these visions did appear. / And this weak and idle theme, / No more yielding but a dream,"* reinforces how the theme of dreams remains all the way until the very end of the play. The narrative of A *Midsummer Night's Dream* draws upon peculiar events and therefore may be disliked by people in the audience. Puck apologises for this by telling the audience to think of the play as their dream.

Q12.

Shakespeare chooses to add this final Act because it allows the character to speak to the audience directly. Although the play has already been concluded (in the previous Act), epilogues are a great way for writers to sum up the main ideas of the play and gain a sense of reaction from the audience.

1. *How does Shakespeare explore different contrasts in A Midsummer Night's Dream? Why are they important?*

- There are many contrasts that you can discuss for this question:
  - o Magic versus normality
  - o Dreams versus reality
  - o Night versus day
  - o Characters behaviour and appearance (Puck plays pranks on characters, whereas Bottom is the victim of the pranks)
  - o Beauty versus ugly
  - o Characters from Greek mythology, English folklore and classical literature

- Whatever contrasts you discuss in your answer, you need to support your answer by suggesting why Shakespeare has used these contrasts. What effect do they have on the audience and how does this tie in with the overall theme of the narrative?

- For example:
  - o The beauty of Titania, who weaves flowers in the hair of the ass-headed Bottom shows two visual juxtapositions.
  - o The fairies are represented as being graceful and magical, which contrasts with the characters of the craftsmen who are clumsy.

QUOTATIONS TO CONSIDER:

"I have had a most rare vision. I have had a dream, past the wit of man to say what dream it was"

- This contrasts the reality with this idea of dreams and visions.

"Base and vile" and "form and dignity"

- How qualities can be transformed.

"We cannot fight for love, as men may do"

- This shows the difference between men and women in terms of love. It shows what women can and can't do in comparison to men.

2. *Why is the title, A Midsummer Night's Dream, important? How does this tie in with the overall narrative of the play?*

- You need to show how the title of the play ties in with the narrative of the play.

- The fact that the play is mostly set during the night, makes the title important.

- The fact that dreams are a significant theme in the play, makes the title important.

- The word 'midsummer' implies how the play is set during the middle of summer.

- You should discuss the importance of the night-time setting in relation to the play. This is where the majority of the events take place. Why do you think Shakespeare has chosen to use this particular setting?

- Discuss the theme of dreams in relation to the characters in the play.

- Dreams occur in the forest which are linked to the unusual, magical events that happen. Show how many of the characters mention dreams throughout the play.

- When discussing dreams, you can also discuss time and how Shakespeare tries to explain unusual events by describing them as a dream.

QUOTATIONS TO CONSIDER:

"I have had a most rare vision. I have had a dream, past the wit of man to say what dream it was"

- This demonstrates the idea of dreams and visions.

"Four days will quickly steep themselves in night, / Four nights will quickly dream away time"

- This shows the themes of dreams and time.

"This old moon wanes"

- Reinforces the night-time setting.

"I'll met by moonlight, proud Titania"

- Again, this shows the setting of night-time.

"Night's swift dragons cut clouds full fast, / And yonder shines Aurora's harbinger; / At whose approach, ghosts, wandering here and there, / Troop home to churchyards"

- Puck is telling Oberon that it's almost dawn.

3. *Explore the nature of love conveyed in* A Midsummer Night's Dream.

- Although this play is not considered a love story like *Romeo and Juliet*, the theme of love is apparent throughout the narrative.

- The play opens with Hippolyta and Theseus discussing their upcoming wedding.

- The play deals with this idea of love and its difficulties.

- Shakespeare presents love as being dream-like.

- Shakespeare uses poetic language throughout the play to emphasise the theme of love.

- Explore the different natures of love between the different relationships in the play. For example:
  - o Hippolyta and Theseus
  - o Lysander and Hermia
  - o Helena and Demetrius

QUOTATIONS TO CONSIDER:

"The course of love never did run smooth"

- Lysander's comment about love and its inevitable complications.

"Four days will quickly steep themselves in night; / Four nights will quickly dream away the time; / And then the moon, like to a silver bow / New-bent in heaven, shall behold the night / Of our solemnities"

- Hippolyta talking to her fiancée, Theseus, about their upcoming marriage.

"Hippolyta, I woo'd thee with my sword / And won thy love doing thee injuries, / But I will wed thee in another key, With pomp, with triumph, and with reveling"

- This implies how Theseus sees love as being conquered as opposed to being romantically enticed.

"Mine ear is much enamoured of thy note; / So is mine eye enthralled to thy shape; Any thy fair virtue's force perforce doth move me / On the first view to say, to swear, I love thee"

- Titania's speech to the transformed Bottom.

THE
REVISION
SERIES

ANSWERS - INTRODUCTION TO POETRY

SONNET 1

Q1.

"That thereby beauty's rose might never die"

"And only herald to the gaudy spring"

Q2.

The words "rose" and "bud" suggests this idea of blossoming. This could be in relation to age, or it could suggest the blossoming of love, and how it is growing.

Q3.

The sonnet explores this idea of human life and time. Shakespeare explores this idea of procreating and continuing legacy through children. The line "but as the riper should by time decrease" is talking about when a parent dies and how the "heir" (their child) will continue those memories.

Q4.

Line two, "that thereby beauty's rose might never die" suggests immortality. If the beauty of a person does not die, it continues to live – through the use of a child.

Q5.

The word "increase" could be talking about an offspring i.e. procreating. The sonnet does draw upon this idea through the line "his tender heir might bear his memory". The use of the words "increase" and "heir" imply similar connotations.

SONNET 116

Q6.

The use of repeated pairs of words suggest that Shakespeare is trying to demonstrate a bond; a couple in love. This allows the theme of love to be explored in the sonnet, which is a common topic for sonnets.

Q7.

Love is presented throughout this sonnet. It is conveyed as part of our physical world. "It is an ever-fixed mark, / That looks on tempests and is never shaken" reinforces how love leaves a huge impact on who we are. The first line of the sonnet: "Let me not to the marriage of true minds" highlights the concept of marital status, and that love will not always be plain-sailing.

Q8.

The structure of this sonnet follows the traditional layout of sonnets. It has 14 lines, which consists of 3 stanzas (a, b, a b), (c, d, c, d) and (e, f, e, f). The last two lines of the sonnet are a rhyming couplet – commonly used to end Shakespearean sonnets. The last two lines of the poem shift the overall tone and mood of the poem with the hope of coming to some resolution. The fact that the poem ends "If this be error and upon me proved, / I never writ, nor no man ever loved," suggests how the poet recognises the possibility of error and therefore everything he has written, would simply be untrue.

Q9.

The line "Love is not love / which alters when it alteration finds" suggests how love will not change even after changes have been made.

Q10.

The use of the star in this sonnet is a metaphor for the love that is explored throughout this poem. Love is compared to the star because, both elements of the physical world are timeless. They can be seen and shared by everyone and therefore implies how love (like the stars) is not restricted by place or time, instead it is something that can be seen and felt by all.

Q11.

Love "bears it out even to the edge of doom" is an extreme statement written with the intention to emphasise just how powerful love can be. This sentence implies how love can conquer all manners of situations.

SONNET 18

Q12.

Sonnet 18 expresses beauty by comparing beauty to nature. For example, Shakespeare compares beauty to a "summer's day"; suggesting how the beauty of that person is "more lovely and more constant" compared to that of summer. The fact that Shakespeare also states: "Nor will you lose the beauty that you possess; / Nor will death claim you for his own", suggests ever-lasting beauty which emphasises the power of love and beauty.

Q13.

The poem begins with a question as it is a great literary technique to quickly draw in the reader. The use of a question makes the reader themselves, question what is being asked, therefore making the poem more interactive and personal.

Q14.

The phrase "the eye of heaven" is talking about the sun. The fact that this poem talks about beauty in relation to nature, reinforces the importance of this reference.

Q15.

The sentence "And often is his gold complexion dimm'd; / And every fair from fair sometime declines" creates visual imagery of sun, beauty and nature. Shakespeare explores how summer eventually fades, just as beauty does as time passes. The fact that summer is 'declining' is compared to his dimmed complexion as a way of emphasising how time changes things.

SONNET 7

Q16.

This sonnet compares the life of a human with the "gracious light" of the sun. Therefore the last word of this sonnet, "son", can be interpreted in two ways. Firstly, Shakespeare could once again be referring to procreating and continuing beauty through generations. Or, the use of the word "son" could be read as 'sun' which symbolises the beauty and light of human life.

Q17.

Religious imagery is conveyed through the choice of words and phrases that Shakespeare has used. The use of the words "sacred," "mortal," "pilgrimage" and "duteous" all carry religious connotations.

Q18.

The last line in this sonnet is significant in regards to the theme of procreating. The sonnet ends with the final sentence: "So thou, thyself out-going in thy noon, / Unlooked on diest unless thou get a son". This implies that, without children, your life would be wasted. Shakespeare highlights the importance of being remembered after death, which can only be achieved if you have a child (and Shakespeare suggests that this child should be a son).

Q19.

When the sun rises in the morning, this signifies the youthful years of the man. As the sun moves through the sky over time, this highlights how time passes, in relation to the sun and age. Once the sun reaches its summit, it begins to fade. This symbolises how people's appearance and age begin to change and draw to a close.

Q20.

This sentence suggests how, once you reach a certain age, you begin to decline in terms of physical appearance and stamina. This is reinforced by the imagery of the sun having reached its peak and light begins to fade.

NEED A LITTLE EXTRA HELP WITH KEY STAGE THREE (KS3) ENGLISH?

How2Become have created these other FANTASTIC guides to help you and your child prepare for their Key Stage Three (KS3) English assessments.

FOR MORE INFORMATION ON OUR KEY STAGE 3 (KS3) GUIDES, PLEASE CHECK OUT THE FOLLOWING:

WWW.HOW2BECOME.COM